IMAGES
of America

BUCKS COUNTY INNS AND TAVERNS

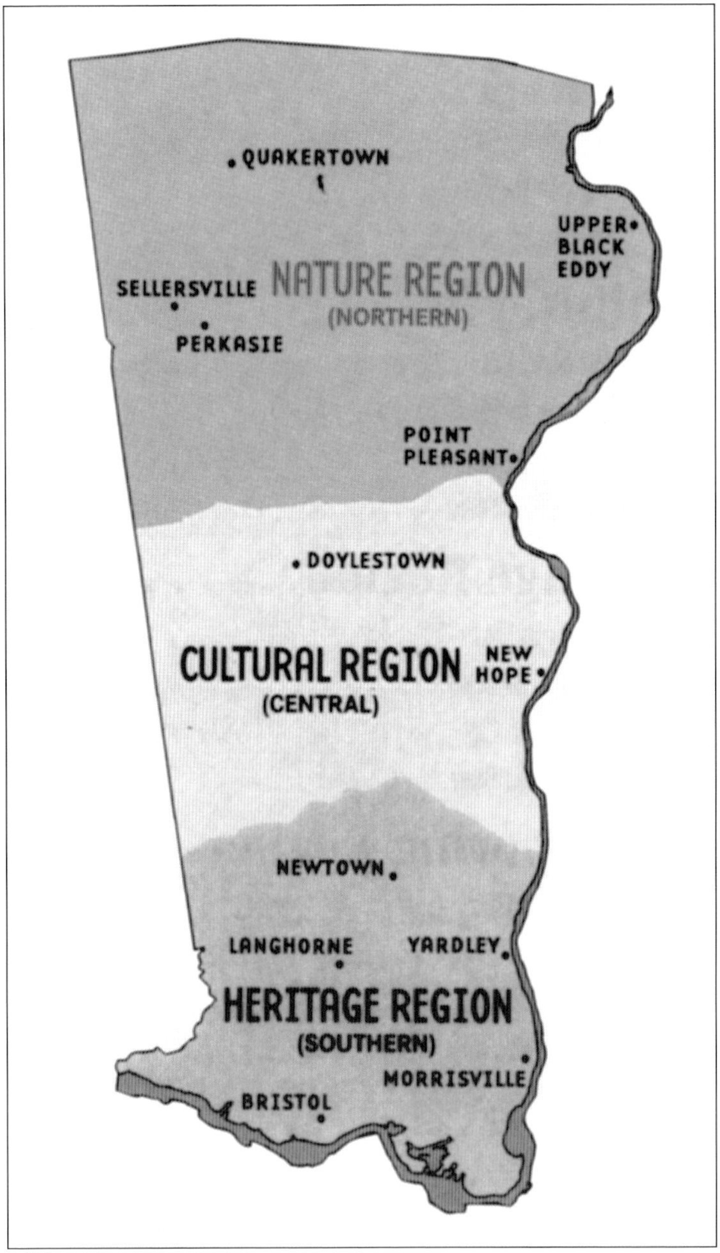

Shown here is a map of Bucks County, Pennsylvania.

On the cover: The Fourth of July was a happy occasion for this patriotic group photographed in the late 1800s at Finland Inn, Milford Township. The proprietors, Mr. and Mrs. A. Schuler stand together in front. Finland, located four miles west of Quakertown, was called the "Poconos of Philadelphia" in the 1920s. Early guests enjoyed hunting and fishing along the Unami Creek (note boot-clad fisherman with creel). It later became a favorite destination for prominent people from the Lehigh Valley. (Courtesy of Rosanna Hein Kern.)

IMAGES
of America

BUCKS COUNTY INNS AND TAVERNS

Kathleen Zingaro Clark

ARCADIA
PUBLISHING

ISBN 978-0-7385-5798-4

Published by Arcadia Publishing
Charleston, South Carolina

Printed in the United States of America

Library of Congress Catalog Card Number: 2008923912

For all general information contact Arcadia Publishing at:
Telephone 843-853-2070
Fax 843-853-0044
E-mail sales@arcadiapublishing.com
For customer service and orders:
Toll-Free 1-888-313-2665

Visit us on the Internet at www.arcadiapublishing.com

Contents

Acknowledgments

The work of regional historians such as the late William J. Buck, W. W. H. Davis, and George MacReynolds inspired me to explore Bucks County and compile this fascinating photographic history. Although I consulted dozens of resources for this publication, I am deeply grateful for the material these gentlemen have passed down as their legacy and for the impact their work has had on my life.

Sincerest thanks go to many people, chief among them my long-time friend Mary Ullman, who gave invaluable editing assistance, and my husband Roger Clark, who provided steadfast support and a sharp eagle eye in the final review process.

Others to whom I am indebted are those who recognize the importance of sharing what they have and know for the benefit of others. To Charles W. Lauble Jr. (Historic Langhorne Association), Gladys Koder (Springfield Township Historical Society), and Edwin Harrington (Solebury Township Historical Society), I thank you not only for the photographs you shared for this book and my earlier release, *Bucks County*, but for the generous gift of your time and knowledge.

Every person or organization that provided an image used in this publication has my profound gratitude, and attributions are listed unless anonymity was requested. My appreciation extends to the many unknown who contributed personal photographs or research to historical organizations to ensure the past not be forgotten.

I especially thank those who assisted, sometimes to a great extent, by sharing collections or reviewing multiple captions for historical accuracy: Betty Riter and Catherine Marek (Springfield Township Historical Society), Iain Haight-Ashton, William Harr (Sine's), William Wheeler (Hulmeville Historical Society), Hilary Jebitsch Krueger (Washington Crossing Historic Park), Sally Sondesky (Historical Society of Bensalem Township), Harold Mitchener (Margaret R. Grundy Memorial Library), Fletcher Walls (Doylestown Historical Society), Jim Maier (Historic Langhorne Association), Heinz Heinemann, Richard Mansley and Harriet Beckert (Newtown Historic Association), Susan Taylor (Yardley Historical Association), Ruth Ehrlen Irwin, Jack Knight, Dorothy McLean, Don Morris, Carol A. Zurick, James Flannery, Ethel Seifert, Linda Jacoby Lippencott, and Earl Hendricks.

And finally, my appreciation goes to those who extended themselves in a variety of ways to help during the photograph collection and research process: Erik Fleischer (Craven Hall Historical Society), Pat Whitacre (Tinicum Township Historical Commission), Chris Handschin (Haycock Historical Society), Evelyn Griga (Margaret R. Grundy Memorial Library), Greg Benscik (Bux-Mont Awards), Kathy Keller (Graphic Energiez), Mike Conti, Joann Whalen, Cherie LaRosa, Joan and Tom Merkel, Lou Bates, Shirley Brady, James Prichard (Perkasie Historical Society), Cheryl Mesko, Mary Ann Sircely, Mary Coleman, Deborah Oxman, Mary Ann Rea, and Phyllis Walton. Bucks County's historical record has been enhanced thanks to all of you.

Introduction

One of the unique features of Bucks County is the abundance of Colonial inns and taverns that have survived into the present. While some are treated with the fond respect accorded an old friend, others are remembered for the prominent place they held in our communities. Even if a distant memory only, these social institutions of sustenance and camaraderie remain accessible through the preservation efforts of many—the entrepreneur, the historian, and those who care enough to preserve the past. It is their work that has made this book possible.

W. W. Davis noted in his 1876 *History of Bucks County* that a tavern in the wilderness was the first sign of advancing civilization. Although early settlers willingly opened their doors to strangers journeying through sparsely populated territory, they were relieved when some enterprising soul proposed a tavern and happily supported that person's license petition to the court.

Initially found at crossroads, ferry landings, creek fords, and turnpikes, an inn or tavern was a welcome sight to weary and weather-battered travelers, despite the unpredictable conditions and incessant inquiries for news encountered inside.

In time, these travelers' rest stops in Bucks County became important gathering places where business was conducted, social occasions were celebrated, and entertainment was provided. They frequently became the news center, polling place, and tax collection site for a village or town, and more than a few, such as the Point Pleasant Inn, evolved into full-scale resorts or first-class hotels. Yet owner turnover and tavern name changes, coupled with a scarcity of photographs and incomplete records, have made it difficult to fully capture the inextricable link between these inns and taverns and community development.

Although Davis reported that Richard Ridgeway was authorized to keep an ordinary (tavern) as early as 1686 in Bucks County's first village, Crewcorne, others such as Gilbert Wheeler were known to have had taverns even earlier and violations are recorded from the beginning, such as those for proprietor Samuel Blakes who was reprimanded in 1703 for allowing "gambling, quarreling and drunkenness" at his establishment.

A fair number of early tavern keepers were well-respected former military officers who became influential members of their communities. Widows also found tavern keeping a viable line of work. Having few other income-earning opportunities, they often kept their families afloat by managing the business after their husbands' deaths, sometimes gaining ownership through a "straw man" (see Bogart's Tavern, page 60).

A significant number of places were witness to historic events such as the American War of Independence and the Fries Rebellion, and many, many were lost to fire, a persistent danger until a century ago. Rebuilt, often bigger and better, several, such as the Anchor Inn and Bensalem's Red Lion, became landmarks by the 1900s only to be lost forever by yet another fire.

British novelist Frederick Marryat commented on America's early-19th-century drinking habits upon visiting in 1839: "If you meet, you drink; if you part, you drink; if you make acquaintance, you drink; if you close a bargain, you drink; if you get elected or lose an election, you drink; if you quarrel or make up," and so on. Yet as far back as 1687 temperance was pledged among members of the Society of Friends (Quakers), who clearly saw the potential damage of intemperance. Several subsequent temperance movements and groups like the Women's Christian Temperance Union ultimately helped rein in unfettered drinking customs.

Whether called an ordinary, hostelry, tavern, inn, or any other name, these social hubs have long provided a place where friends meet, business is transacted, and relationships are forged. They have been an integral part of our past and will forever be a part of our future, and a great deal of both ordinary and extraordinary life will continue to take place within their walls.

One

Lower Bucks Heritage Region

Before William Penn was granted the province in 1681, the enterprising Dunk Williams had already established his ferry on the Delaware River. An inn was operating at the site by the early 1730s. In 1834, the riverfront property was sold containing 238 "beautifully situated" acres and a two-story "Stone House . . . occupied as a Tavern and Ferry House." Dunk's Ferry Hotel, Bensalem Township, became a popular shad-fishing and duck-hunting resort in the mid-1800s and is now part of Neshaminy State Park. (Courtesy of Joanna Kranansky, artist.)

This *c.* 1690 Newtown home, known as the "Old Frame Tavern" until 1817, is the oldest frame building in Pennsylvania. In 1723, Agnes Welsh, who had many mouths to feed and an imprisoned husband, sought a tavern license so she could continue to operate her "house of entertainment." The tavern witnessed several Revolutionary War events and was still dispensing "liquid joy" when it became the Bird-in-Hand in the early 1800s. (Courtesy of Historic Langhorne Association, Ed Vogenberger Collection.)

Few know that long before Lower Buck's Hospital, Silver Lake, and the Eagle Diner, land in this Bristol vicinity was part of America's earliest resort spa, Bath Springs. The heyday for this celebrated 30-room hotel was late 1700s to early 1800s, when many prominent citizens and foreign visitors enjoyed the spa's curative waters, fancy dress balls, and horse races. Amenities included gourmet meals, a wine cellar to suit "Bacchus's hoard," and special accommodations for "domestics." (Courtesy of the collection of the Margaret R. Grundy Memorial Library.)

Bristol's Ferry House (King George II Inn), established in the late 17th century on the Delaware River, accommodated travelers journeying between New York and Pennsylvania or Maryland. In 1768, Charles Bessonett "bought the Ferry House and inn" according to license records. He later established a noteworthy stage line. Many wealthy visitors to the Bristol Springs spa stayed here, as did early presidents and dignitaries seeking "refined hospitality." It was long promoted as America's oldest continuously operating inn. In 1827, great crowds watched a procession of engineers and laborers with tools, spades, and wheelbarrows march to the groundbreaking ceremony for the Delaware Division of the Pennsylvania Canal. As part of this "jubilee occasion," officials banqueted here to toast the project destined to create many fortunes. The late Joe Cuttone, a barber in his 90s, fortunately preserved many Bristol images including the one below. (Above, courtesy of the collection of the Margaret R. Grundy Memorial Library; below, courtesy of Joseph Cuttone.)

When the landmark Anchor Inn, Wrightstown Township, was built around 1724, locals were finally relieved from being awakened at all hours by travelers seeking shelter. It was a favorite meeting spot for county residents. Early-20th-century Doylestown mayor Dan Atkinson fondly recalled the Anchor of his childhood as the place to leave the carriage and warm up on cold winter trips to Newtown. (Courtesy of the Historic Langhorne Association, Ed Vogenberger Collection.)

The Old Anchor Inn's Wrightstown Township location made it a fine spot for the elections and cattle auctions once held there. In 1975, its advertisements noted the inns' offerings: "Good old-fashioned American food in a country setting. Cocktails served. Lunch a la carte from $1.25. Dinner a la carte from $4.95." It was purportedly the oldest continuously operated tavern in the county until destroyed by fire in 1998 and replaced by a pharmacy. (Courtesy of Jim Maier, Historic Langhorne Association.)

Washington Crossing State Park's Old Ferry Inn (formerly McKonkey's) sits on the embankment of the Delaware River where Gen. George Washington and his Continental army crossed on Christmas night in 1776, launching the Revolution's pivotal Battle of Trenton. Above, secretary of Pennsylvania's Department of Forest and Waters Maurice Goddard explains the site's history in 1966. The inn was used a year later (below) by the Daughters of the American Revolution (DAR) for an event honoring Pennington United Methodist Church's pastor Rev. Rollo Michael (seated). The DAR, descendants of those who helped America achieve independence from Britain, including soldiers who once encamped here, raised funds to preserve this historical property. Note the original Colonial wicket bar that could be closed to protect stock when the barkeep was not present or to protect the barkeep himself if customers became too unruly. (Courtesy of Washington Crossing Historic Park, Pennsylvania Historical and Museum Commission.)

Nancy McMinn, bartender and an original owner of the *c.* 1772 Temperance House, likely cooked meals for her guests in this still-used fireplace. Both she and her husband, Andrew, were described by historian Josiah Smith as quite "fond of whiskey." Their Newtown tavern, which included an addition where Andrew taught school, later operated as a temperance house serving ginger pop, mead, and mineral water. Subsequent Temperance House names included the Good Samaritan and Niagara Temperance House. (Author's collection.)

The Clovernook Inn, Cornwells, was located on Williams Avenue near Bristol Pike. During World War I, men employed by the Traylor Shipyard to build wooden ships stayed here during the week, returning to families on weekends. Clovernook subsequently became a home for boys and later an apartment house. (Courtesy of the Historical Society of Bensalem Township.)

When Art Ridge bought the Newportville Inn in 1981, he was following in the footsteps of ancestor Walsmley Ridge, who operated Bensalem's White Horse Tavern in the early 19th century. Art and his family renovated the early-18th-century structure, originally a miller's home, adding an outdoor dining deck and a restaurant section. In the early 1800s, it was a club for "fashionable" young men from Philadelphia. It ultimately became a tavern around 1865. (Courtesy of Art Ridge.)

The White Bear Tavern, licensed in 1811, helped give Richboro its original name, Beartown. It was a popular meeting spot for politicians. In 1821, the proprietor Enoch Addis formed a voluntary militia—the Alert Light Horse Company. The inn, under the name Spread Eagle, was closed in May 1994. Major preservation efforts by the Northampton Historical Society resulted in this landmark being saved and moved slightly south. It now houses a business. (Courtesy of Warren Williams; photograph by Arnold Brothers.)

Stage drivers would head for the nearby Old Stone Tavern after dropping riders at Bensalem's renowned Red Lion Inn as it was improper to overnight where passengers stayed. The building, over 200 years old, is now the Eddington Presbyterian Church Manse. A ferry near the inn (once also called the Bloomsdale Ferry House) was used by Vice Pres. Aaron Burr when he fled to New York in 1804 after killing Alexander Hamilton in a duel. (Courtesy of the Historical Society of Bensalem Township.)

Amos Strickland built the original portion of Newtown's Brick Hotel around 1763 on Washington Avenue, once a well-known racecourse called Strickland's Lane. Joseph Archambault, a former officer of Napoleon Bonaparte, purchased it in 1829, modernizing and enlarging the building into a first-class hotel. He initially worked as both dentist and hotelkeeper and later became a real estate developer and Civil War cavalry officer. Today lodgers and guests seeking a refined dining experience still patronize this former stagecoach stop. (Courtesy of the Brick Hotel.)

After her father, John Shelly Wright, a prominent Middletown Township citizen, died of a sudden heart attack in 1909, Mabel and her bartender husband, C. Taylor Knight, began operating the Langhorne House (now Joseph's Garden Grill), built around 1876 by her grandfather Frederick. These two photographs show the transformation from new building to successful hotel. During its heyday, vacationers seeking respite from the city disembarked at the train station across the road and found immediate refreshment and accommodation. The saloon in the rear was entered from the side of the building, while the front was used as private quarters. The hotel was later sold outside the family, but Jack Knight recalls his grandfather Caleb taking him there as a boy and treating him to "peanuts and a soda." The barn behind the attached carriage shed was used as a local polling place. (Courtesy of the Historic Langhorne Association.)

This Bellevue Avenue building, an educational institution for 40 years, became a popular summer resort in 1875. Located on the northeast corner of Bellevue and Winchester Avenue, Langhorne, contemporary advertisements touted the "view of a beautiful country for many miles . . . well shaded lawn of over four acres . . . 160 feet of piazza," plus boating and fishing along the "romantic Neshaminy." Special "conveyances" were available to take guests to Bristol's famous Paxson's Spa Spring. (Courtesy of the Historic Langhorne Association.)

After the Revolution, chief financier Robert Morris became a senator in the newly formed United States government. His proposal that the capital be established near the Falls of the Delaware (Morrisville) lost by only two votes. Subsequently his name was given to both the town and to the Robert Morris Hotel at Bridge Street and Delmorr Avenue (formerly Mill Street). The hotel's tavern sign was painted by distinguished folk artist Edward Hicks (1780–1849). (Courtesy of James and Jane Murray.)

Rachael Jackson's 1768 license for Bristol's Clossen House was the earliest documented license for this hotel, although historian Doran Green noted that documentation was lacking for earlier public houses. In 1857, William Earley, citing a shortage of overnight accommodations for canal boatmen, triumphed over considerable opposition to license his Exchange Hotel here. It became Closson, with an *o*, in the early 1900s and was also once known as the Keystone. (Courtesy of the collection of the Margaret R. Grundy Memorial Library.)

The Court Inn, whose early-18th-century trade was bolstered by Newtown's nearby courthouse, retains much of its original structural accoutrements such as wide-plank floors, window and door frames, moldings, and wrought iron hardware. When Joseph Thornton began building his tavern (above, left) in 1733, he used brownstone obtained from local quarries and a stylish Flemish bond brickwork design. After Joseph's death in 1754, his wife, Margaret, continued their "Public House of Entertainment" until at least 1776. Although the hostelry ceased operations in 1800, the building was still called Thornton's Tavern in the 1960s. Since then an earlier, more romantic name, Half-Moon Inn, has been reinstated. The southern portion (on right) was purchased after the north building (on left with flag) and $25,000 for restoration was donated to the historical society by Robert and Ruth LaRue in 1964. Both sections may be toured. (Courtesy of the Historical Society of Bensalem Township.)

In the late 19th century, Brennan's Hotel in Eden (now Penndel) was a desirable vacation spot near Hulmeville Park, the Neshaminy Creek, and Parkland. It was located at the corner of Park and Centre Avenues by the railroad station. The building, barn, and sheds were leveled in 1940 to make way for the Enterprise Wallpaper Mill. (Courtesy of the Historic Langhorne Association.)

Before being demolished in the 1950s for the Pennsylvania Turnpike, LaTrappe was one of the oldest in the county. Built in the 1700s, it was named for a French bear trapper who lived on the Poquessing Creek. The Historical Society of Bensalem Township possesses the inn's beautiful Victorian-era china set. An old hotel guest list includes many early Bucks County names, including Tomlinson, VanSant, Vanartsdalen, Vandergrift, and Bennett. (Courtesy of Warren Williams; photograph by Arnold Brothers.)

Bucks County's first public road, the Kings Highway, had existed for over a decade by 1686, when it converged with other early roads in Bristol. This late-17th-century "Market Town" became county seat 1705, the year of its first tavern license petition. The Coleman House was one of 10 essential hostelries established during Bristol's first two centuries. The bell tower of Bristol's first town hall is visible in this early-1900s photograph. (Courtesy of the collection of the Margaret R. Grundy Memorial Library.)

Hulmeville's Old Colonial Hotel was originally John Johnson's creamery, where cheese, butter, and other dairy products were produced. It is believed that the building was constructed in the early 19th century. Called the Dutch Club after it opened as a bar in the 1940s, it drew local men for beer and cards for many years. Originally part of Hulmeville Park, today Liberties Bar and Restaurant offers beautiful views from its large outdoor dining deck. (Courtesy of the Hulmeville Historical Society.)

Samuel Slack's temperance house, erected in 1845, became a tavern when licensed by his son Aaron 22 years later. Today owners of Yardley's newly refurbished Continental Tavern are proud of its interesting history. Customers and workers of the neighboring gristmill and bargemen delivering coal were among its earliest patrons, and its location near the Delaware River and canal made it an ideal stop on the Underground Railroad. Fugitive slaves were reportedly hidden here before being transported to Quakertown, where Richard Moore, a potter and Quaker leader, would help them continue their clandestine journey to Canada. In 1876, Slack's growing complex was destroyed by fire after a tenant barber overfilled the stove while disposing of his day's shearing. The rebuilt hotel is shown above when streets were unpaved and below when rooms could be had for 75¢ per night. Neither image is dated. (Courtesy of Frank Lyons.)

Flannery's bar (above) on Route 1 in Penndel was owned by Anna Flannery, who purchased the restaurant here in 1939 after operating Parkland's Paris Inn for 11 years. The spittoon near customer Bill Hewins was among those still found in rural area taverns in the 1940s (others disappeared during World War II scrap drives). Anna and her son Jim expanded the building in the mid-1950s (below) to accommodate banquet facilities, a new bar, and a growing business. In 1967, Jim brought in a 1954 Lockheed Super G Constellation from Capitol Airways and converted it to a distinctive cocktail lounge that included an attractive wooden parquet dance floor. After the landmark property was sold in the late 1990s, the retired plane was relocated to the Air Mobility Command Museum in Dover, Delaware. (Courtesy of the Historic Langhorne Association.)

Although Flannery's is largely remembered as the famous U.S. Route 1 landmark seen above, it was born of humble origins. In 1939, after failing to acquire the Parkland restaurant she had been operating since 1928, the widowed Anna Flannery bought the Wunch Brothers restaurant (seen behind the bus in the photograph below). At the time, Penndel was still called South Langhorne, and her son Jim was a teenager. By 1951, the pair had expansion plans. On October 11 that year, they had the building on the right relocated to another part of their property and enlarged the restaurant, adding banquet facilities and a bar. After his mother passed 16 years later, Jim, by now a retired pilot, acquired the *O-Five-Charlie*, a retired Lockheed Constellation, for a cocktail lounge, which became a popular destination night spot. (Courtesy of the Historic Langhorne Association.)

The Buck Hotel, a prominent meeting place for centuries, was once especially popular with influential politicians. Many significant social and cultural events, both local and national, were celebrated at this landmark. It was a polling place, stagecoach stop, and relay point for changing horses. Its clever, decades-old advertising motto, "Don't Pass the Buck," is still used, although the days of standing room only at the Old Bar are a distant memory. (Courtesy of the Historical Society of Bensalem Township.)

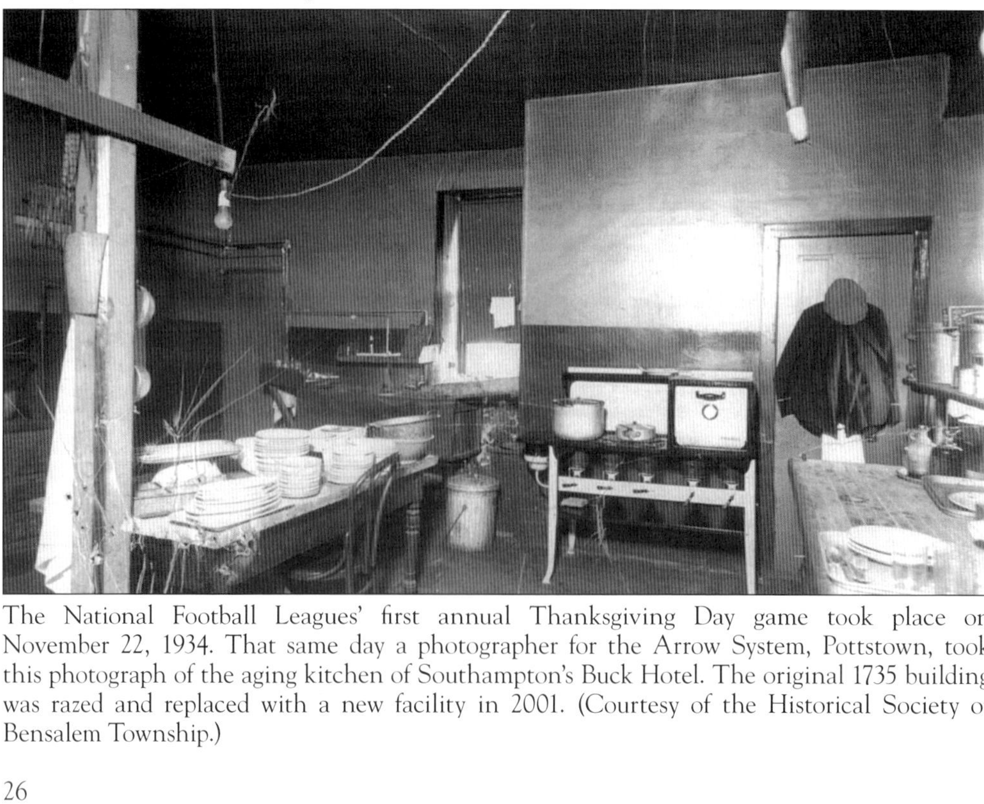

The National Football Leagues' first annual Thanksgiving Day game took place on November 22, 1934. That same day a photographer for the Arrow System, Pottstown, took this photograph of the aging kitchen of Southampton's Buck Hotel. The original 1735 building was razed and replaced with a new facility in 2001. (Courtesy of the Historical Society of Bensalem Township.)

The first marketing promotions for the Langhorne Manor Hotel, a popular summer resort built 1889, described "twenty-six acres of the finest land," open lawn, towering oaks, a three-acre lake fed by "a cool sparkling spring," wide piazzas, and a delightful view—all "truly first-class." The building later housed the Foulke-Long Institute for Orphaned Girls, then St. Mary's Manor, a Catholic educational institution. Today a new building hosts the Philadelphia Biblical University. (Courtesy of the Historic Langhorne Association.)

The Yardley Inn (other names included Ferry House, Cryan's, and White Swan) is located where Benjamin Fleming's *c.* 1790 tavern operated when Yardley's Ferry was in service. A raft landing was located just south, where East College Avenue terminates today. Riverside tavern keepers who delivered food and drink by rowboat to the rafters likely included Fleming and his successors. These 1950s hunters pose at the inn with their kill, including a 500-pound bear. (Courtesy of the Yardley Historical Association.)

Johnny Apples Bar and Restaurant, Holland, opened in October 2003 and has been recognized in a national magazine for its famous martinis. The original building, erected in 1724, served as a general store for many years and is shown above looking north on Buck Road. The Finney family owned and operated both the store and the gristmill across from it for eight decades. The building also once housed a post office and served as a gas station. The Rockville covered bridge, deemed too small for automobiles, can be seen in the process of being dismantled in the 1932 photograph of the station below. The bridge was located just south of the building and accommodated many travelers heading to the landmark Buck Hotel, a highly popular meeting place and hotel for almost three centuries. (Courtesy of the Historic Langhorne Association.)

In 1911, Bristol historian Doran Green described how Benjamin Blinn opened a temperance house in 1838 but that "like all other temperance hotels opened in Bucks County, it died for want of patronage." While probably an exaggeration, it is true that Blinn's place closed and later became the Cottage Hotel, then in Green's time, the Silbert House. Pictured here around the 1920s, this building now houses Annabella's, a cozy Italian restaurant. (Courtesy of the collection of the Margaret R. Grundy Memorial Library.)

This sketch of the Old Ford Inn, by Joanna Krasnansky, captures the days when Colonial travelers crossed the Neshaminy in a flatbed ferry. Today the stunningly transformed Salem Creekside Inn (located along Bristol Pike below Croydon) retains its spirit of the past along with its original hardware, doors, and windowpanes. Lore is that John Hancock's signature was etched in a bookcase door pane, now gone, when he, George Washington, and Marquis de Lafayette stayed there. (Courtesy of Historical Society of Bensalem Township.)

William Penn began building his home in Fallsington Township in 1682, but Fallingston's first tavern did not open until 116 years later in 1798. At different points it served as a stagecoach stop, library, jail, general store, post office, lodge hall, and hardware store and hosted a traveling circus in the yard. The Stagecoach Tavern (other names included Fallsington Inn and National Hotel) resides in a former Quaker village little changed over the centuries. (Author's collection.)

Only the original undated stone section of Morrisville's Hoagland House survived construction modifications on its way to becoming a present-day commercial bank. Located at East Bridge Street and Pennsylvania Avenue, it has been used for a variety of commercial purposes since the 1920s. Morrisville became home to Bucks County's first settlers in 1624 and missed becoming the nation's capital by only two votes in 1783. (Courtesy of James and Jane Murray.)

Despite a devastating fire and diverse businesses housed here, the reconstructed Whitehall Hotel building looks relatively the same as it did 100 years ago. Photographs from the 1880s, several decades before it was known as Keith's Hotel, show gas lighting installed in 1858 by the Newtown Gas Light Company. Today adjacent carriage sheds help evoke earlier times of this former inn and tavern licensed in the mid-19th century. (Author's collection.)

Not all taverns operated according to regulations. One reported mid-18th-century tavern keeper of Richboro's Black Bear got into a bit of trouble because "he had no regard to the laws, encouraged drunkenness, gaming, fighting, etc., on week-days and Sunday" and "doth frequently abuse and beat his wife in an extraordinary manner." This popular gathering spot for 18th-century politicos started as a log cabin and was destroyed by fire. (Courtesy of Warren Williams; photograph by Arnold Brothers.)

Finney's Mill on Buck Road in Holland was built 1787 and like other mills in Bucks, found new life as a restaurant in later years. It became the Mill Race Inn in 1962. It was seriously damaged during Hurricane Floyd on July 30, 2000, and ravaged again by a flood nine months later. To date it has not reopened. (Courtesy of the Historic Langhorne Association.)

Washington Crossing Inn, Taylorsville, was just one of many inns and taverns that began as a family homestead (above). The oldest portion of the farmhouse, on the right, was built around 1817–1821. It was originally owned by the Taylor family, which operated the nearby ferry in the 19th century after the McKonkey's. The walk-in working fireplace of the original kitchen now provides charming Colonial atmosphere to this upscale dining establishment. The Decker and Sine families are shown below in 1889. Their home was converted to a restaurant after William and Bertha Haven purchased the property in 1932 and relocated their establishment from the nearby historic building known today as the Old Ferry Inn. (Courtesy of Marc Elliot.)

In 1723, plantation owner Evan Harris accommodated so many travelers along King's Road that he decided a tavern was necessary. Philip Amos assumed tavern keeping duties in 1730, but his death led his wife, Ann, to take over just five years later. She eventually purchased and enlarged the streamside property, operating Widow Amos's until her own death in 1758. This well-known stagecoach inn (its image was captured on Philadelphia's Walnut Street Theater curtain drop) became Bensalem's landmark Red Lion. Constitutional Convention delegates including John and Samuel Adams were guests, and George Washington's troops camped here on the way to Yorktown. In 1930, just after the Hall family (1845–1929) sold the business, it was padlocked for liquor law violations. It reopened after Prohibition (shown below enlarged, 1960s) but was destroyed by arson in 1991. George Fridel, above, was hostler (horse groom) during the 1890s and early 1900s. (Above, courtesy of Betty Luff; below, courtesy of the Historic Langhorne Association, Ed Vogenberger Collection.)

The Langhorne Hotel, originally a hipped-roof, brick-and-stone building with a log kitchen, accommodated travelers as early as 1704. In November 1743, the *Pennsylvania Gazette* advertised it as a "two story dwelling house . . . now being a tavern (at) four Lane-Ends, Middletown." Later the first store located above Bristol would open here. The hotel became a significant part of the area's development with the advent of the railroad in 1876. George Ehrlen took over the Langhorne Hotel in 1905. His daughter, Ruth, recalled "a busy place employing chefs, waitresses, upstairs maids, a laundress, seamstress and bartenders." The large barn, "a huge wagon and carriage house," stable yard, and Holstein cow (to supply milk and cream) were cared for by hired help and a hostler who also watered stabled horses or met guests at the railroad station in a carriage or sleigh. (Courtesy of the Historic Langhorne Association.)

In 1780, for "Two Silver Dollars, or the exchange in Continental," Gershom Johnson's "Stage Waggon, commodiously fitted for passengers" would take a northbound traveler from Philadelphia's Sign of the Bunch of Grapes to Princeton. The first overnight stop was here at Four Lanes End, 22 miles away. The Langhorne Hotel has had various names over the years, including the Blue Grotto, the Sign of the Black Horse, and the Farmers' and Drovers' Inn. (Courtesy of the Historic Langhorne Association.)

This Langhorne Hotel Victorian-era guest room far exceeded accommodations found in Colonial days when a traveler was fortunate to find a bed to share with a stranger. In the early 20th century, this premier hotel provided guests with telephone service, transportation to and from the railroad station, a hostler, and stables for their horses, plus fresh milk and cream provided by a resident Holstein cow. (Courtesy of the Historic Langhorne Association.)

Ruth Ehrlen Irwin, 97, daughter of Langhorne Hotel's proprietor George Ehrlen (operated 1905–1935), recalls long-term boarders and overnight travelers dining together in this room photographed around 1914. When linemen were in the area installing telephone and electric lines and boarded here, their lunches were personally delivered to the job site by George. Hidden behind the paneling was a beautiful redbrick fireplace with a bake oven, which George uncovered to the delight of his family and guests. (Courtesy of the Historic Langhorne Association.)

Comparisons of these two photographs illustrate how many old Colonial taverns were transformed over two centuries. The side view of McKonkey's Tavern Ferry House, which overlooks the Delaware River in Taylorsville, is shown above with white plaster, later removed to expose the original fieldstone construction so common in Bucks County. The small rear building (right in both photographs) is the original tavern built before 1750 by Samuel Baker, who began the ferry here during the late 1600s. The larger front portion resulted from additions made between 1814 and 1854, decades after George Washington dined here with Gen. Nathanael Greene and Gen. John Sullivan before the 1776 Battle of Trenton. The Old Ferry Tavern (a later name) is no longer in operation. It is now part of Washington Crossing Historic State Park and is open as part of its guided tour. (Above, courtesy of Jim Maier, Historic Langhorne Association; below, courtesy of Marc Elliot.)

The beautiful gardens, sophisticated service, and tasteful decor have attracted visitors to the Washington Crossing Inn since the early 1930s, when William and Bertha Haven relocated their restaurant to this location. The original sign hung by the Havens (seen right in above photograph) was found and reinstalled in the mid-1990s by then owner Frank A. Cipullo. The c. 1817 kitchen is now one of several warmly decorated dining rooms, as is the enclosed sunny porch inlaid with brick. Known for its fine cuisine and attention to detail, today this stately historic building adjacent to Washington Crossing Historic Park hosts many elegant weddings and celebratory events. The unidentified elderly ladies at right enjoy the sun on the inn's deck in the mid-20th century. (Courtesy of Marc Elliot.)

Over two centuries old, the present-day Hulmeville Inn is a well-established "corner bar," whose patrons represent a broad cross-section of people. Like many such taverns, it has long provided a convenient, comfortable meeting place for locals and community organizations and sponsored many local sports teams. The community-oriented proprietor Jeff Lavin, president of the Bucks County Tavern Association, notes that longtime customers can recall coming to this neighborhood mainstay with their fathers. Meanwhile, bartender Jackie Clemens-Meyer, a 20-year employee, can recall fascinating encounters with tavern spirits of another kind. Established 1803 by town founder, mill owner, assemblyman, and first president of the Bank of Bucks County, John Hulme Jr., the inn has a long history reflecting one of its slogans, "Good Times, Good Food, Good People." The photograph above was taken prior to renovations announced below by the new owner in 1896. (Courtesy of Jeff Lavin.)

OPENING.

You and your friends are cordially invited to attend the opening and inspection of the improvements made at the

HULMEVILLE HOTEL,

Saturday, October 24th 1896.

A Flag Raising will be held at 5 O'Clock, P. M.

Good Music will be in attendance.

The Hulmeville Hotel was erected around 1803 by the highly respected town founder John Hulme Jr. to accommodate travelers on the increasingly busy route between Trenton and Philadelphia. Although he presided over a growing town with many visitors, he built the hotel without a barroom and prohibited the sale of alcohol. Subsequent owners reversed his policy. The Mareks opened a café and ice-cream shop (above) at this former stage stop during Prohibition. Upon repeal of the act, they converted the business to a bar and grill with upstairs apartments. The Mareks owned the business for 70 years (1924–1994). Severe hurricane weather flooded their property (below) along with many others in 1955. (Above, courtesy of Jeff Lavin; below, courtesy of the Hulmeville Historical Society.)

The family of dry goods store founder Justus Clayton Strawbridge, a Quaker, enjoyed traveling in their tallyho (coach drawn by four horses) to the Langhorne Hotel for a "country meal." The family used this photograph for a 1915 Christmas calendar. Business for this bustling place soon started to decline with the sequential challenges of World War I, Prohibition, the rerouting of Lincoln Highway (Maple Avenue), and discontinuance of the trolley. (Courtesy of the Historic Langhorne Association.)

Two

Central Bucks Cultural Region

In the early canal days, bargemen gathered at New Hope's *c.* 1794 River House to drink, gamble, fight, and sleep it off before starting another day. One legendary proprietress, a 300-pound woman named Madge Featherstone, reportedly could brawl with the best of them. In 1961, former musical comedy star Odette Myrtil (she performed as Bloody Mary in Broadway's *South Pacific*) opened Chez Odette's, a highly popular French bistro, cabaret, and piano bar. (Courtesy of Ted Nichols; photograph by Hampton Hayes.)

The Waterwheel, above Doylestown, started as a remotely located gristmill in the 1720s. Owner John Dyer successfully lobbied for a road to connect his mill to provincial governor William Keith's property (Graeme Park, Horsham). The resultant Dyer's Mill Road eventually became an important artery—Easton Road. The inn, photographed by Milton Rutherford, became a popular hangout in the 1940s and 1950s for stars and celebrities such as James Cagney and Dorothy Parker. (Courtesy of Rutherford's Camera Shop.)

Wilbert Duvall, proprietor of Pineville Tavern, proudly stands behind the bar he owned and operated from 1948 through 1962. After he moved his family from Montgomery County into upstairs quarters, his children began attending the local one-room schoolhouse. The Abruzzese family presently operates this busy tavern along with its adjoining restaurant. Long a community gathering place, an old-time congenial atmosphere and comfort food are still found within its walls. (Courtesy of Richard Duvall.)

Noisemakers, party hats, cigarettes, pretzels, and of course, drinks, were staples of New Year's Eve parties in the mid-20th century. Here grocer Harry Neld and Vi Eller, owner of the local hamburger joint the Wagon Wheel, celebrate the coming of a new decade on December 31, 1959, at their friends' pub, the Pineville Tavern. Note the poster behind the couple announcing the ever-popular Thursday night special, spaghetti and meatballs. (Courtesy of Richard Duvall.)

In 1948, when Wilbert Duvall purchased Pineville Tavern, licensed in 1732, it shared the first floor with a Unity-Frankford grocery store. Outbuildings included a feed store, barbershop, horse barn, wood shed, and two outhouses. Gas pumps and a porch-side water pump also remained. Wilbert's son, Richard, recalls farmers meeting on the lot to transfer milk to a creamery truck, and an old trapper who bought and sold animal pelts from his Chevy. (Courtesy of Richard Duvall.)

On September 21, 1897, the *Trenton Times* reported that just below Montgomery County's Horsham Hotel (near the Bucks border) "shanties for laborers" laying the trolley road were being erected and that when completed, "cars will leave Doylestown and Willow Grove every fifteen minutes." This period photograph shows old and new overlapping. Notice the outhouse, water pump, gas lantern, and old washtub, as well as telephone and electrical lines and a sign for the "trolley waiting room." (Courtesy of Warren Williams.)

In 1830, New Hope's Logan Inn was servicing Bucks County's "only manufacturing town" located near a ferry connecting the two most populous counties in Pennsylvania and New Jersey. Former guests of this present-day fine-dining establishment and inn ranged from famous Colonial figures to stage personalities of the 20th century. Begun in the 1720s, it advertises as "Bucks County's oldest continuously run inn" and as one of the five oldest in the United States. (Courtesy of the Historic Langhorne Association, Ed Vogenberger Collection.)

Solebury's first covered bridge over the Delaware River, built in 1814, eliminated the need for John Reading's century-old ferry. It was later replaced (bridge in both photographs) then destroyed by fire in 1923, a scene captured by Pennsylvania impressionist and eyewitness Edward Redfield, in his renowned painting *The Burning of Centre Bridge*. The year the first bridge was erected, a nearby c. 1761 tavern sustained fire damage and was reconstructed, becoming Painter's Ferry Tavern. Additional conflagrations caused the tavern to be rebuilt twice in the 1900s. After the second inferno, it rebounded quickly and reopened in 1960 as the Centre Bridge Inn. Advertisements for the new facility promoted "mid-week dinners for $1.95 and Frank Bartholomew's hip keyboarding." Today this elegant hotel replicates Williamsburg style and provides fine dining, charming guest rooms furnished with antiques, and a river view. (Courtesy of Jerry and Tina Horan.)

The abandoned home pictured here on Devils Half Acre, a strip of land between River Road and the Delaware Division Canal, was never an official tavern or inn. The site presumably received its moniker from activities that took place here as early as 1792. George MacReynold's (*Place Names in Bucks County*) noted that canal builder reports written between 1828 and 1832 indicate that "whiskey was sold without license and the place became the scene of drunken revelry."

When photographed for this 1940s postcard, the Old Cartwheel Inn, opened around 1796, was touted as "Known from Maine to Florida on Route 202." Travelers enjoyed "delightful guest rooms," outdoor service, a cocktail lounge, and two dining rooms offering classic mid-20th-century fare such as homemade biscuits and steak with waffles. It later became a popular nightspot and was New Hope's only dance club when damaged by fire in 2005. It was recently demolished. (Courtesy of Ted Nichols.)

Lumberton's *c.* 1758 "house of public entertainment" (left end, above) was possibly its first. Around 1819, tavern keeper Samuel Runk's landlord claimed "hard times" as his excuse for not providing a tavern sign. Runk decided to make his own. According to writer Thaddeus Kenderdine, Runk dipped a stick in tar and "streaked" the words "Hard Times" across an old shutter he then suspended. The name stuck. Kenderdine's Aunt Elizabeth became landlady and hostess of the Hard Times Tavern in 1834, when he noted she was "fighting the battle of life"—newly widowed with an infant and child. She renamed it the Camel, and Thaddeus reminisced about jamborees loud enough "to scare the rats from under the cellarless floor." It closed in 1841, when Elizabeth moved to Philadelphia. When Bucks impressionist William Francis Taylor (1883–1970) purchased the property, he sketched the romantic image below. (Above, courtesy of Newtown Library Company; below, courtesy of Phyllis Taylor Euhler.)

The Conti family expanded their busy restaurant three times between 1954 and 1962. The original mid-18th-century Cross Keys Tavern building (above) was retained as a small, intimate dining room with a Mercer-tiled fireplace, and was photographed in the mid-1950s, a few years after Walter Conti joined his parents, proprietors Frank and Emily (Walter's sons Joe and Michael joined the family business later). A rear addition (below) provided modern dining facilities and a bar. Innovative cuisine, savvy marketing, and events such as wine tasting established the Conti Inn as a famous upscale dining destination. Its white table linens, internationally influenced fare, and European-style service attracted a diverse clientele from businesspeople, professionals, and civic leaders to writers, theater celebrities and Philadelphia families taking a weekend country drive. (Courtesy of Walter Conti.)

It has been reported that King George loyalists met at the Cross Keys Tavern during the Revolutionary War. In the late 19th century, the hostelry was called Drover's Inn, a bow to its then clientele. It operated until 1906, when its license application was rejected, and then reopened after Prohibition, providing overnight accommodations once more. Frank and Emily Conti (right) became proud owners during the early 1940s. They discontinued lodging, and little knew their Plumstead "saloon" would one day evolve into one of the most profitable restaurants in the United States. As a young immigrant, Frank had worked as dishwasher, busboy, waiter, and ultimately restaurant manager. This experience, combined with Emily's northern Italian recipes, successfully launched the renowned Conti Inn, operated by the family until closing in 1995. (Courtesy of Walter Conti.)

Walter Conti's hard work and dedication to his business and trade helped bring Bucks County national recognition. Conti's Inn experienced phenomenal growth and national fame after he assumed leadership for the family restaurant in 1965. He has been recognized for industry excellence and has held numerous distinguished ancillary posts, including president of the National Restaurateurs' Association, president of the Pennsylvania Restaurant Association, and chairman of the Culinary Institute of America. (Courtesy of Walter Conti.)

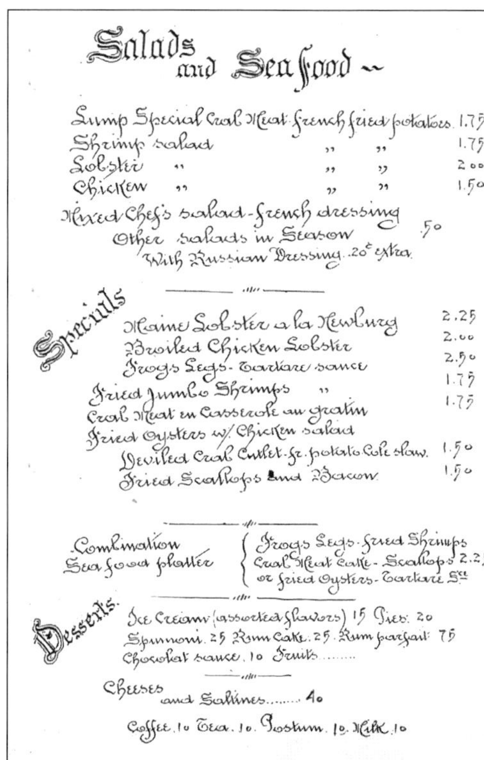

Salads and Sea Food ~

Lump Special Crab Meat french fried potatoes 1.75
Shrimp salad " " 1.75
Lobster " " " 2.00
Chicken " " " 1.50
Mixed Chef's salad - french dressing
Other salads in Season .50
With Russian Dressing 20c extra

Specials
Maine Lobster a la Newburg 2.25
Broiled Chicken Lobster 2.00
Frogs Legs - Tartare sauce 2.50
Fried Jumbo Shrimps " 1.75
Crab Meat en Casserole au gratin 1.75
Fried Oysters w/ Chicken salad
Deviled Crab Cutlet - fr. potato Cole slaw 1.50
Fried Scallops and Bacon 1.50

Combination Sea food platter { Frogs Legs - Fried Shrimps, Crab Meat Cake - Scallops 2.25, or fried Oysters - Tartare Sce

Desserts
Ice Cream (assorted flavors) 15 Pies 20
Spumoni 25 Rum Cake 25 Rum parfait 75
Chocolate sauce 10 Fruits ....

Cheeses and Saltines 40

Coffee 10 Tea 10 Postum 10 Milk 10

The Conti Inn menu eventually grew from this hand-drawn mid-20th-century version to one with over 100 items. Before cosmopolitan tastes demanded it, Conti's served only free-range chicken, locally grown vegetables, and the freshest of fish supplied daily—nothing canned or frozen. Little wonder they grew from a 40-seat pub to a 300-seat dining room with frequently long lines of hungry patrons craving Conti's succulent soft-shell crabs, luscious mussels, or steak au poivre. (Courtesy of Walter Conti.)

Carverville's Hillside Home and Pleasure Park opened in 1859 as a coeducational high school, the Excelsior Normal Institute. In 1873, William Evans turned it into a year-round spa resort with "Magneto-Electricity, Vital Magnetism, Electro-Thermal and Medicated Vapor Baths." Newly refurbished rooms, luscious gardens, and recreational activities, including billiards and bowling, drew guests from as far away as Europe and South America. After Evans's death, it briefly became a tuberculosis sanitarium and then a children's orphanage. It was demolished in 1939. (Courtesy of Edwin Harrington.)

Buckingham's Ottoway House burned down during 1936 renovations two weeks before its scheduled reopening. To save neighboring homes, firefighters resorted to a bucket brigade and pumped dry the pond near the intersection of Old York Road and Buckingham Pike. Named by prominent politician George W. Ott, also a "well-known Doylestown cattle dealer," this hotel, dating back to at least 1860, was popular during the days of the Swift-Sure Stage Line. (Courtesy of Jim Maier, Historic Langhorne Association; photograph by Arnold Brothers.)

Fireside dining in the winter and al fresco dining in the summer made the Tow Path House one of the most romantic restaurants in New Hope in the late 20th century. The internationally influenced menu was complemented with authentic Italian cuisine whenever proprietor Paul Licitra's mother, Christina (born in Foggia, Italy), visited. Diners were often treated to live music that ran the gamut from chamber music to cabaret. (Courtesy of Paul Licitra.)

New Hope's Tow Path House, reopened in 1980 by Paul Licitra and Warren Troust, was part of a canal-front complex with quite a past. In the early 1800s, an oyster house and general store shared the lot with adjacent bordellos (one for the gentry, one for barge workers). A hollowed space beneath the front porch purportedly hid Canada-bound slaves traveling the Underground Railroad. Besides a fortune teller and alleged ghosts, the intriguing but unconfirmed names Bucket of Blood and Cesspool Annie's for an early inn and restaurant, respectively, add to the property's legend. Under Licitra and Troust the terraced restaurant (today *TUSCANY at the Towpath House*) attracted celebrities such as Jack Lemmon, Grace Kelly, and Julia Child, to dine by its rustic copper-hooded fireplace. (Courtesy of Paul Licitra.)

This *c.* 1758 building was once a stagecoach stop between Philadelphia and New York. Bucks County painter and preservationist William Francis Taylor, the first president of the Delaware Valley Protective Association, purchased the riverfront building in the early 20th century and opened the Cuttalossa Inn. Located in the nationally registered Cuttalossa Valley Historic District, its cascading waterfalls and natural surroundings have provided a charming creek-side setting for both dining and weddings for decades. (Courtesy of the Historic Langhorne Association, Ed Vogenberger Collection.)

The 18th-century Plow (presently Gardenville Hotel, rebuilt around 1871) had several interesting connections to the notorious Doan Gang. Historian William Buck reported claims that Moses Doan once "sprang from between his guards over a low covered wagon . . . and thus escaped" from its porch. Col. William Hart, alerted to a Doan hideout while drinking here in 1783, formed a posse that killed Moses Doan during a subsequent shoot-out. J. H. Battle's *History of Bucks County* noted several Doans were buried from here. (Courtesy of Cecelia and Jim Hyrsl.)

William Francis Taylor, a founding member of the artist community that launched the celebrated New Hope art colony, painted the illustration above of New Hope's Delaware House. Taylor was a leader in forming the Phillips Mill Community Association, raising the funds to purchase the mill property for the artists known today as the Pennsylvania Impressionists. The Delaware House, on Bridge and Main Streets, was built around 1818 and accommodated those journeying between Philadelphia and New York via Old York Road, one of the oldest stage routes along the East Coast. First called the Union Hotel, it was built by William Maris, a prolific builder of homes, shops, mills, and mansions, of which several still remain. The bridge seen in the early-1900s photograph below was originally a covered bridge built around 1814. The Delaware House is presently a coffeehouse serving the tourist trade. (Above, courtesy of Phyllis Taylor Euhler; below, courtesy of Ted Nichols.)

This tavern at Cross Roads, as Hartsville was initially called, was erected in 1742 and was once the scene of much activity, including cattle auctions. Nearby was land that became an encampment site for 13,000 of George Washington's soldiers in 1777. Col. William Hart, who formerly served as proprietor of the Plumsteadville Inn, opened his Sign of the Heart tavern in the building shown. These two views capture the Hartsville Hotel, as it was later known, during its final days. Pictured above are Kathy and Larry Hannon in 1964, approximately nine months before the aging building was taken down. Their mother, Ruth Hannon, photographed neighbors gathered to watch the building's demolition. A local gentleman, Elmer Rinck, saved the well. (Courtesy of Rick Parker, Inc.)

Doylestown's landmark inn, rendered above by Bucks County impressionist William Francis Taylor, began in the mid-18th century as William Doyle's tavern. The original tavern was confiscated during the Revolution after the subsequent proprietor joined the British army and was arrested for "high treason." Between 1815 and 1836, several expansions resulted in an upstairs ballroom, a third-floor addition, 30 guest rooms, a double piazza, and a 60-horse stable. A local once recalled "large shipments of western horses" selling here. When proprietor William Corson replaced the well in 1872 with a fountain, he renamed this stagecoach stop Fountain House. In 1928, proprietor Francis Mireau hosted the Great Fountain House Antiques Sale. This notable occasion drew approximately 1,000 "important people" to Mireau's 4,000-lot collection, and many items were acquired for the DuPont, Ford, and Mercer museums. This prominent historic building presently hosts a coffeehouse. (Above, courtesy of Phyllis Taylor Euhler; below, courtesy of Rutherford's Camera Shop.)

During the Revolution, Bogart's Tavern (also known as General Greene's) was headquarters for Bucks County's first Committee of Safety and meeting place for field officers from other county companies. After Mary Jamison purchased her deceased husband's tavern through a "straw man" in 1767, she and her second husband, John Bogart, spied on customers and annoyingly reported innocuous conversations to the committee. In 1901, historian Warren Ely postulated that Bogart's had "witnessed the birth and evolution of this great nation." (Courtesy of the Historic Langhorne Association, Ed Vogenberger Collection.)

This is an early view of the former stagecoach stop Carversville Inn. When built 1813, it was named Bird-in-Hand; the town was called Milton (likely short for Mill Town). Thomas Carver became proprietor in 1844 and renamed it Carversville House. Modified to Carversville Hotel in 1854, it operated as such until the days of Prohibition. This cozy dining establishment has been known as the Carversville Inn since the 1950s. (Courtesy of Ned Harrington.)

The North Penn Railroad launched a branch on its Philadelphia–Bethlehem line on October 6, 1856, by sending the *Civilizer*, a locomotive with "two passenger coaches," to Doylestown. That same year, Enos Kulp's "eating stand" became Walford's Hotel, renamed the Railroad House Hotel in 1861. A daily 6:00 a.m. whistle announcing the train's impending departure sent guests scurrying. Enlarged in 1896 and open until 1946, it was later demolished to create a parking lot. (Courtesy of Rutherford's Camera Shop.)

The Black Bass possesses an impressively rich heritage and has long provided authentic Colonial surroundings and beautiful Delaware River views. Sections date from the 1740s, and its fabled history includes rambunctious canal men and Tory sympathizers. It contained a bar from Maxims in Paris and was handsomely decorated with British royal memorabilia. Although it succumbed to floods in 2007, new owner Jack Thompson restored and reopened the restaurant, bar, and guest rooms in 2009. (Courtesy of the Historic Langhorne Association, Ed Vogenberger Collection.)

It has been over 150 years since the Fountain Inn served as a public house. Opened before 1835, it gave its name to the surrounding village located near Doylestown. The inn was situated near a large spring fed by several artesian wells where water rose above the ground "like a fountain." Not surprisingly, the inn enjoyed piped water, a benefit from its proximity to the spring, and adorned its sign with a fountain. (Author's collection.)

Allen Heist purchased the original early-19th-century building on this site—the Court Inn— in 1866. He replaced it with this larger brick building and renamed it the Monument House in 1883. It was located across from the county courthouse and Civil War monument in Doylestown. In the 1920s, it promoted a "splendid menu" and "Ample Garage Facilities." Subsequently renamed the Bucks County Inn, it was demolished in 1964. (Courtesy of Rutherford's Camera Shop.)

Before the Heins (pictured) became proprietors of the Doylestown Inn in 1920, the hotel was one of several in town with a livery stable where travelers such as salesmen delivering goods could rent a horse and wagon. During the 1938 centennial, the inn was advertised as Doylestown's "most modern hotel," boasting "every room with bath." The Jug in the Wall basement tavern once attracted many renowned writers and theater celebrities. (Courtesy of Rutherford's Camera Shop.)

The 14-room, c. 1900 Wycomb Hotel, Wycomb Pub & Grill today, was part of a resort enterprise envisioned by civic-minded entrepreneurs Charles and Emma Thompson Cope (Charles owned and operated similar resorts in Atlantic City and at the Delaware Water Gap). Nearby they added guest cottages; fishing, boating, and recreational areas; a barbershop; and a dance hall with shops below. Weekly auctions and snapper soup specials (turtles supplied courtesy of the local boys) were big hits. (Courtesy of Warren Williams; photograph by Arnold Brothers.)

This lovely Ranulph Bye watercolor captures the spirit of the planned Victorian community envisioned by the entrepreneurial founder and developer of Ivyland, Edwin Lacey. Although a quaint borough (one of America's smallest today) eventually arose from 40 vacant acres, Lacey's planned Temperance House Hotel was a failed project and financial disaster. It never opened as a hotel and became a private summer home instead. It now houses apartments. (Courtesy of the Historical Society of Bensalem Township.)

In 1761, Kungle's Tavern identified both a village and its tavern, being named after the tavern proprietor George Kungle. The village eventually became Chalfont. This building, the Chalfont Hotel, replaced the original structure following a fire in 1903. It was designed by Oscar Martin, a Drexel alumnus. Martin, who was influenced by the arts and crafts movement, also designed many prominent homes in the region. The building is now Borgi's restaurant. (Courtesy of Marilyn Becker.)

Three

Upper Bucks Nature Region

The Ottsville Inn was a late-19th-century gathering place and watering hole well patronized by farmers and drovers moving produce and livestock to market. This charming photograph of the costumed proprietor and an unidentified but obviously happy group was taken around 1960. At the time it was not completely uncommon for children to visit the local taproom with their dads. Today the Ottsville Inn serves authentic Italian cuisine in a warm, upscale atmosphere. (Courtesy of Filippo Mignano.)

When private rooms were scarce, the Richland Centre Hotel would have been a welcome find. Edwin Sheetz opened it 1856 with "six bedrooms and six beds" for train travelers. Four years later, taxes were assessed at $450. When Henry Ahlum became proprietor in 1876, it was called the Eagle Hotel. In 1950, it advertised having "the charm of colonial times . . . home cooked food . . . excellent rooms . . . and [as being] removed from the noise" of the railroad station. (Courtesy of Gladys Koder.)

Bursonville Hotel (later White Horse Inn) opened 1807 and was operated by Isaac Burson until 1843. Springfield researcher June Barron Griffith reported that rural Bursonville was the "home of stills during Prohibition." Pleasant Valley resident Ethel Seifert recalled "plenty of stills" and bootleggers "cooking moonshine" were in her area too, and Earl Hendricks, whose grandfather owned the East Rockhill Hotel, grew up hearing stories about an E. Rockhill still from his father. (Courtesy of Gladys Koder.)

In the late 18th century, Michael Swartz (later anglicized to Black) owned a tavern near his ferry on the Delaware. A century later, Lower Black's Eddy Hotel (subsequently called Mountainside Inn and then the Mountain House) stood in its place. It was a popular spot for loggers to tie up, rest, and for $5, to find a more experienced steersmen to take their raft downriver through the difficult Wells Falls in New Hope. (Author's collection.)

Before becoming the Quakertown Moose Lodge around 1921, 115 East Broad Street had been home to David Neidig's Continental Restaurant for at least 27 years. Neidig provided lodging by day or week, and his advertisements promoted "First-Class Accommodations for Commercial Men." Notice the shoe shine stand, barbershop pole, livery entrance, and, at lower left, the sign advertising next-door neighbor, "house and sign" painter Fred H. Fluck. The upstairs porch and covered entrances were added after 1894. (Courtesy of Gladys Koder.)

In 1807, Adam Romig opened a tavern that became known as the White Horse Inn. In 1830, proprietors John and Elizabeth (Hess) Knecht gave up the hotel because of competition from the new Springtown Inn. They subsequently kept "open house" in their home for young people in the community, however. In 1920, Harvey and Addie Strock purchased the property and established the highly successful Strock Farms selling meats, produce, and vegetables. (Courtesy of the Springfield Township Historic Commission.)

Walter Baum, author of *Two Hundred Years* (1938), wrote, "Though there is no supporting data available, I have a firm belief that Clemmershteddle was the original name of Sellersville." If so, the earliest patrons of this tavern licensed in 1753 would have known of this early moniker for their German community. After 25-year-old Samuel Sellers bought the tavern in 1790, he and his family established a reputation for providing "very comfortable accommodations," and like many other proprietors, a willingness to barter for produce. In the 1800s, customers checked their guns at the bar (stored in drawers seen); by the 1970s they were riding their motorcycles through its restaurant. And although the tavern's subsequently replaced front bar was smashed to pieces by officials during Prohibition for violations, today the restored Washington House, resplendent with its c. 1900 back bar (above), antique decor, and Victorian atmosphere, is far removed from such raucous days. (Courtesy of William Quigley.)

The affable Molly Smieciuch presided over the once prosperous Bedminster Hotel, general store, and ice-cream shop for over 50 years, retiring in her late 80s. She and her husband, Emil, bought the place in 1939 to serve locals and travelers along the 46-mile Route 113. Their daughter Christine recalls respectful customers—"no excessive drunkenness or cursing like today"—but remembered if a farmer got a bit too "tipsy," her father would drive him home. Decades before, in the brick barn (below) behind the hotel, livestock auctions took place downstairs and World War I uniform pants were produced in the Fretz factory upstairs. In the 1940s and 1950s, workers could buy a soda and lunch platter consisting of hamburger, mashed potatoes, and peas for 35¢ at the hotel, and on birthdays, Fretz factory foreman Mr. Vance treated employees to cake and Breyer's ice cream in the ice-cream shop. (Courtesy of Christine Myers.)

The Elephant's original post-mounted sign (dated 1848) surely elicited a sigh of relief from weary travelers passing through Bedminster. The historic hotel, sold in 2002 by Dolly and Lou Lokay, was family owned for most of the 1900s. A patron recalled its last days as a "shot and beer" place where unsanctioned billiard competitions took place and an "adopted" fawn once wandered among customers. The Elephant's tavern and restaurant are planned to reopen in 2011 after renovations. (Courtesy of the Historic Langhorne Association, Ed Vogenberger Collection.)

Wayfarers traveling Old Bethlehem Pike or Durham Road through Springfield Township converged at Opp's Tavern (above), where both roads intersected above Springtown. German pioneer and former Revolutionary War captain Valentine Opp noted in his 1790 license application that he had already kept his public house "for a considerable time past." During the war, Opp had raised the Flying Camp company, one of four from Bucks County. Like many retired military officials, he later became an innkeeper. He also became a member of the Pennsylvania legislature and contributed to relief efforts to help Philadelphia during the disastrous 1793 yellow fever epidemic. His son, Valentine Jr., inherited the tavern in 1797 but in 1816 purchased the Farmers' Inn (later Clear Spring Hotel) in Doylestown's Germany section (north of courthouse), which was family operated for 27 years. William Franklin Quier (below) was a mid-20th-century property owner. (Courtesy of Kenneth W. Quier and Verna Quier Klotz.)

As seen in these photographs from the Spinnerstown Hotel, some bar patrons in the early 1940s were perfectly content to sip beer, munch peanuts, and beat their buddies at cards, while others preferred to wager outdoors. Card playing and footraces were a common means for early taverngoers to win drinks or money. According to Alice Morse Earle in *Stage-Coach and Tavern Days*, officials have attempted to prohibit such wagers and gaming since the time of the Puritans when magistrates prohibited "carding, dicing, tally bowls, billiards, slidegroat, shuffle-board, quoits, loggets, [and] nine-pins," which were "not deemed reputable at the ordinary." (Courtesy of Susan and John Dale Jr.)

The construction of the North Pennsylvania Railroad between Philadelphia and Bethlehem began in 1853. By 1854 a hotel was completed to accommodate travelers in Bridgetown, a community integrated into Perkasie in 1898. Called the South Perkasie Hotel, it was widely known for its livestock auctions and by 1929 equally famous for its monthly Saturday afternoon outdoor market. Today patrons of the Perk enjoy food and drink in a lively setting surrounded by a plethora of vintage photographs. (Courtesy of Larry Nacarella.)

Point Pleasant Inn, a famous resort at the dawn of the 20th century, proudly promoted pilsner beer, a *c.* 1842 Austrian creation particularly favored by German immigrants. This robust golden lager arrived the same time mass-produced clear drinking glasses began replacing wood, leather, and ceramic steins. Its visual appeal and taste quickly made it preferable in both Europe and America over its dark and cloudy counterparts. Philadelphia brewers C. Schmidt and Sons (1860–1987) produced 100,000 barrels of beer in 1892, including pilsner, "the world's first golden beer." The two large broadsides advertising Schmidt's Puritan and pilsner beers below indicate Point Pleasant Inn's saloon was among many watering holes keeping the Schmidt's company busy. The saloon was located in the front west end of the building, which now houses attractive decorative items for F. P. Kolbe's fascinating home goods, garden, and gift store. (Courtesy of Rebecca and Richard Kolbe.)

While drovers headed for city markets found the significant grazing farm near the Applebach Hotel ideal, travelers appreciated Henry Applebach's "large and accommodating" inn and its shed, stable, and carriage house for their horses and vehicles. An 1890 *Intelligencer* article described this hotel as being "the best the country round," and locals later enjoyed square dances here. This former stagecoach stop, renamed White Hall Hotel, was painted by artist Dennis Gerhart from a *c.* 1900 photograph. (Courtesy of Jane Nase.)

This antiquated former stagecoach stop, the Red Hill Inn, served Ottsville (also known as Red Hill), a community established in the early 1700s. Although it may have been in operation earlier, John Fry is recorded as petitioning for his tavern license in 1804. In 1917, Stacy Weaver recalled that fights between the Straus Gang and its rivals occurred here in earlier days. James Emery placed the commemorative "Walking Purchase" marker (far right) in 1900. (Courtesy of Lyle Rickards.)

Capt. Nicholas Buck's late-18th-century blacksmith and wheelwright shops on Durham Road, Nockamixon, fostered growth of "a thriving German community," which became Bucksville. Buck founded the Washington Light Horse cavalry around 1807. It trained on his property, known for its magnificent mountain views, for decades. He operated a tavern as early as 1809, and 25 British soldiers were held overnight here in 1814. It later became an important mail stage stop, post office, and general store, and language and music classes were conducted here at one time. In 1840, Bucks's son Nicholas Jr. erected a new building, the White Horse Hotel. A sign over the bar read, "IITYWYBAD," an acronym for "If I tell you, will you buy a drink?" Today the authentically decorated and reportedly haunted Bucksville House transports guests back to another time. Buck family descendants include historian William J. Buck and several tavern keepers. (Courtesy of Barbara Szollosi.)

YOU ARE RESPECTFULLY INVITED TO ATTEND

A GRAND SOCIAL

Picnic at the Bucksville Hotel

—ON—

FRIDAY AFTERNOON AND EVENING, JULY 1ST, 1881.

FLOOR MANAGERS: GODFREY BUCK, WM. HEANY, JOHN ATHERHOLT.

GENERAL MANAGERS.

JERVIS SMITH, BISHOP HEANY, JORDAN HEANY, FRANCIS HAGER, WILLIAM SHUPE, HENRY HELLER.

MUSIC BY DOAN'S ORCHESTRA

If the weather be unfavorable, to be held on Saturday afternoon and evening, July 2, 1881.

J. H. Battle's history noted that Riegelsville, located on land once an island in the Delaware River, got its start when Benjamin Riegel erected a large stone barn in 1814 and then a "commodious house" in 1820 from which he operated a tavern. With the canal completion in 1832, he envisioned several moneymaking opportunities. He built a hotel and had 24 building lots surveyed for sale. Today the historic town and Riegelsville Inn bear his name. (Courtesy of Gladys Koder.)

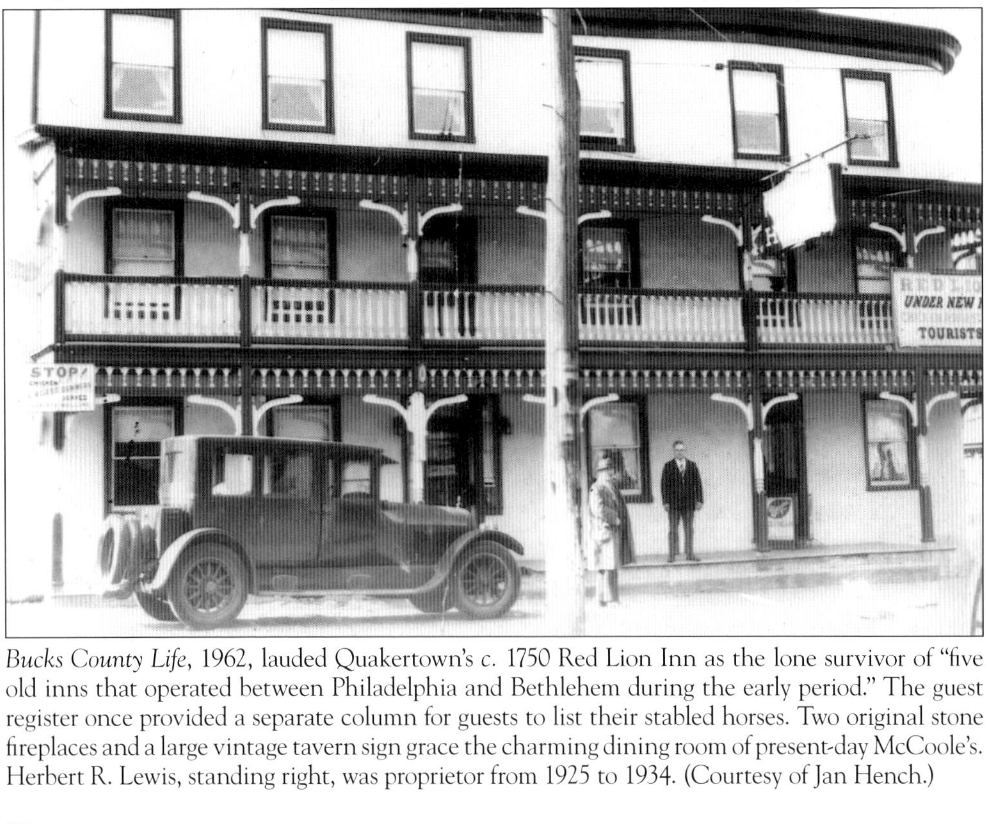

Bucks County Life, 1962, lauded Quakertown's c. 1750 Red Lion Inn as the lone survivor of "five old inns that operated between Philadelphia and Bethlehem during the early period." The guest register once provided a separate column for guests to list their stabled horses. Two original stone fireplaces and a large vintage tavern sign grace the charming dining room of present-day McCoole's. Herbert R. Lewis, standing right, was proprietor from 1925 to 1934. (Courtesy of Jan Hench.)

This undated photograph of the Springfield Township's Zionhill Hotel (built 1820) shows its water pump in a wooden casing to protect it from the elements. The tavern and early stagecoach stop was located on Old Bethlehem Pike (a former Native American trail) and became an ice cream, candy, and tobacco store after it was acquired by William P. Lucas c. 1905. It was later converted into a double home where his descendants lived until 1962. (Courtesy of Gladys Koder.)

Frederick Heany, Hagersville Hotel tavern keeper around 1795, was a leader in the 1799 tax rebellion with fellow auctioneer John Fries. By the 1870s, Hagersville, named for Perkasie's founder Samuel Hager, was a significant business center with mail delivered by stage triweekly. In the 1920s, there were call girls at the hotel. A local senior citizen related that men would "find (this) out for themselves" when they went there at the urging others. (Courtesy of the Historical Society of Bensalem Township.)

The original *c.* 1855 section between the towers of the Bush House was erected to accommodate travelers on the North Pennsylvania Railroad. When the hotel opened under the Sign of the Quakertown Station, Quakertown was little more than a 62-home village. Although William H. Bush owned the hotel for only 19 years (1863–1882), it still bears his name. Outfitted with a ballroom, the Bush House advertised in 1910 as the "Finest Equipped Hotel in the Country." (Courtesy of Gladys Koder.)

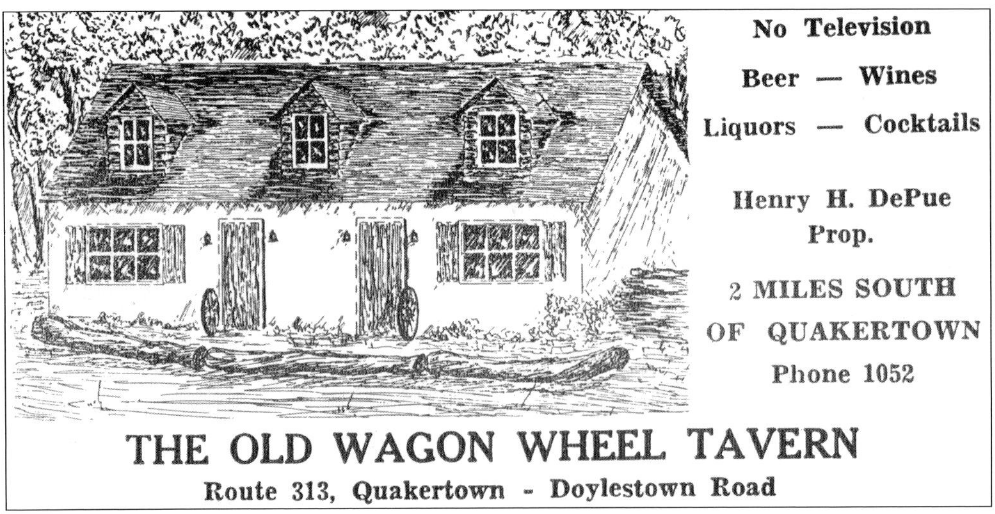

While cameras in intimate public spaces may irritate today, in the 1950s, people were annoyed by the incursion of television into their public retreats. The Old Wagon Wheel Tavern below Quakertown proudly highlighted "no television" in this 1953 *Bucks County Traveler* magazine advertisement. The pub later became known for what has been described as "um-pa" music (polkas) played by the late, classically trained "one-man band," Rollie Fretz, the former owner of Fretz's Music Center.

Erwinna's *c.* 1857 Golden Pheasant Inn is the only continuously operated mule-barge stop on the Delaware Canal. A stopping place for lodging, beer, and salt cakes during earlier rough-and-tumble canal days, this charmingly elegant French country restaurant and antique-filled bed-and-breakfast belies such humble origins. This highly romantic dining destination is on the National Register of Historic Places and within a short drive of five covered bridges. (Courtesy of Barbara Faure.)

The Ottsville Inn on Old Durham Road is located in a Tinicum Township village once called both Ottsville and Red Hill. Erected in the early 1870s by Thomas Harpel, a popular proprietor, it was preceded by the Red Hill Inn, a former stagecoach stop on Easton Road. The Ottsville Inn became a trolley stop in 1904, and residual cobblestone pavement from those days is still visible in front. It is presently a fine Italian restaurant. (Courtesy of Filippo Mignano.)

Ferndale, below Kintnersville, was once a thriving community with several boot and shoe manufacturers that served the mining industry. Historian Willis Rivinus noted that local old-timers knew the former stage stop here as Rum Corner. Today the fine fare and tasteful decor of the Ferndale Inn (center, around the 1920s) continues to woo customers to what was once "a local joint." (Courtesy of Ferndale Inn.)

This former stagecoach stop, the Ferndale Hotel, began operating as an inn around 1830. These front and side views were taken around 1915. The above photograph includes an unnamed neighborhood girl who identified herself to the proprietor in her senior years while visiting the present-day restaurant here. The others pictured may include family of proprietor Claude A. Traguer or guests staying in the "tourist rooms." Dinners advertised in the late 1930s could be had for 50¢, 75¢, and $1 and included steak, "chops," and chicken. In 1957, hotel advertisements in the *Bucks County Traveler* promoted "county hams from nearby farms [and] home-baked pies." Today the Ferndale Inn continues the tradition with appetizing entrees and homemade desserts. (Courtesy of Ferndale Inn.)

This 1920s view of Springtown's main street shows Pleasant Valley Hotel between Isaac Shelly's general store (with gas pump) and Calvin Bleem's garage. The excellent road condition was likely the result of the Springtown road improvement league formed by residents in 1910. Bleem's garage, erected in 1920, was one of many newly-built garages in the region (there were 2,000 in Philadelphia alone by 1926) to serve the fast-growing driving public. (Courtesy of the Springfield Township Historical Society.)

The 1871 *Bucks County Gazetteer* described Richlandtown as "a considerable village . . . at the end of the Turnpike road" with "a hotel, a large store, cigar manufactories, and a fly-net manufactory." Today the Richlandtown Inn, a former stagecoach stop established in 1812, promotes "superb cuisine" and retains many interesting historic features, such as a tin ceiling, Chinese-inspired leather wallpaper, and a beautiful Victorian mahogany and oak bar that was made in Allentown and delivered by wagon. (Courtesy of Mary Ferrara.)

The handlebar-mustachioed proprietor of the Pleasant Valley Hotel, William C. Link, stands at the ready before customers arrive, around 1906. Weekenders arriving by "hay ride" from other hotels were once welcomed to organized sauerkraut dinners here. The finely crafted bar, tin ceiling, and well-used spittoon evince a typical barroom scene from this era. Previous names for the hotel include Snyders, the Centennial, and Pleasant Hill. (Courtesy of the Springfield Township Historical Society.)

Pleasant Valley Hotel began in 1801, and early names included Pennsylvania Coat of Arms, Pennsylvania Arms, and the American Arms. Nine proprietors subsequently operated it under the Sign of the Black Horse Inn. Residents paid their taxes (including dog taxes) and voted here. In 1856, it received a remonstrance for serving spirits. It was destroyed by fire in the early 1900s. Later a reportedly not-so-secret house of ill repute operated in the vicinity. (Courtesy of the Springfield Township Historical Society.)

John Wilson, grandson of Ralph Wilson, who traded with the Lenni Lenape Indians, licensed the Harrow Inn in 1744. Flanking doors provided separate entrances for men and women, while inside the stone fireplace heated the men's section only. In 1783, one traveler reported supper "very good" but the "people dirty, the house swarming with bugs." Subsequent proprietors developed a pleasant eating and drinking establishment from this earlier stagecoach stop in Nockamixon Township. Stan and Helen Przyuski (left) owned 65 acres encompassing the tavern (below) for several decades in the early to mid-1900s. Helen operated the business alone for a decade after Stan passed away in 1949. Strictly religious, she substituted a tuna salad sandwich whenever Catholic patrons ordered meat on Fridays. "Chef Tell," television's pioneer chef, later owned a restaurant here. It is presently a real estate office. (Courtesy of Stan and Terry Przyuski.)

The Point Pleasant Inn in Upper Bucks was a popular Pocono-like retreat that attracted large groups, families, and sports enthusiasts to its lovely environs between the Delaware River and the Tohickon Creek. Its large staff was housed across the road in a three-story brick building with 12 bedrooms exclusively assigned to the help, some of whom are pictured in this playful scene with their boss, believed to be Charles C. Housem. (Courtesy of Rebecca and Richard Kolbe.)

Ernest and Paula Knuth (Paula is above center with glasses) employed the open sky, rolling hills, and cascading springs of a former 17th-century manor in Upper Bucks to create a pastoral retreat for city folk. They opened Kintnersville's Cascade Lodge in 1939 and began promoting their "Home for Quiet and Rest" near the Delaware River. Introductory accommodation rates in this pre–Revolutionary War farmhouse were $6 per weekend and $18 per week, including meals. Summer recreation included swimming (below), fishing, tennis, quoits, and archery, while winter offerings included ice-skating, "skeeing," and tobogganing. Enthusiastic visitors from Philadelphia and New York enjoyed the amenities and communal dinners into the late 1950s, when the inn discontinued lodging. Today patrons enjoy stunning panoramic views and delight in watching wonderful gourmet meals prepared table-side by executive chef John Wolf, a PBS culinary guest, and his staff. (Courtesy of Howard Knuth.)

Young Howard Knuth (above, right) and his mother, Paula, assumed proprietorship of the Cascade Lodge following his father's death in 1953. Several years later, this country retreat obtained a liquor license and became a fine-dining establishment. At its peak in the 1960s, its renowned restaurant served as many as 400 dinners on a Saturday night. The bar, equally lucrative, served on average three-plus drinks per person. Celebrities such as Meryl Streep and Billy Joel have counted among well-known guests. The Cascade Lodge's distinctive setting (below) includes a spring-fed trout pond (fresh trout is a specialty), grazing Arabian horses, and gorgeous views—a perfect backdrop for banquets and weddings. The warmth of an open-pit fireplace and surprise horse-drawn sleigh rides add to the enjoyment of this truly unique establishment come winter. (Courtesy of Howard Knuth.)

The North Penn Restaurant, Quakertown, sat opposite the depot where Broad Street intersected with the North Pennsylvania Railroad tracks. It was purchased by Henry Neidig from George Moser in 1904 and licensed to sell beer. Its signs and advertisements declared "Meals at all hours" and "Oysters in every style." The first-floor tavern had been known to locals in more recent times as the Texas Bar. Rooms were available above. (Courtesy of Gladys Koder.)

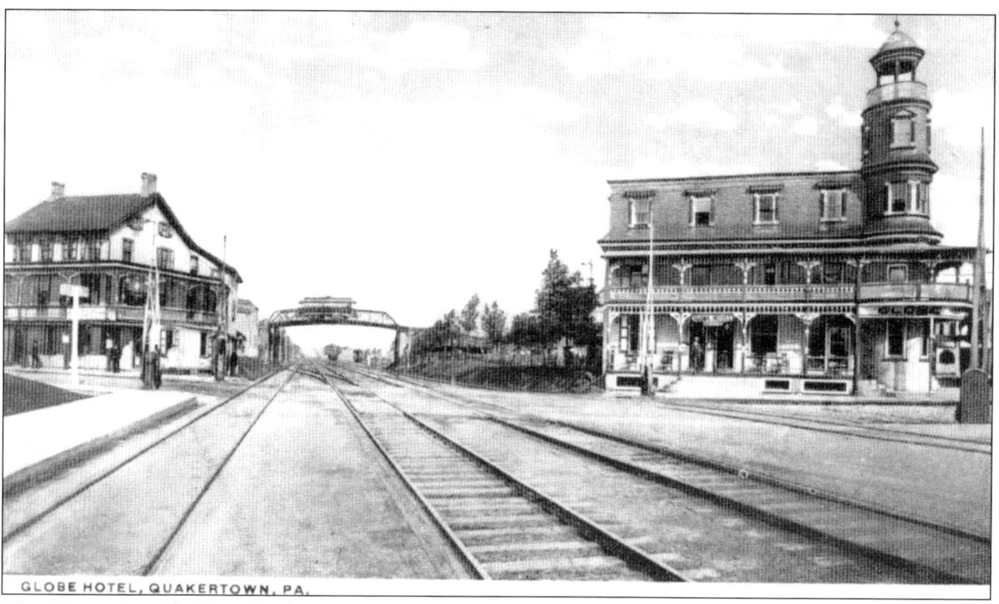

The Texas Bar (left) and Globe Hotel (right) straddled the Quakertown tracks over which the "tripper" may be seen crossing via the railroad bridge. Operators of this "new-fangled horseless bus" were forbidden from entering a saloon in uniform, and teetotalers were given hiring preference. The 5¢ trolley was bright red, ran from 7:00 a.m. to 12:00 p.m., and had a cow catcher described as big enough to "cope with elephants as well as cows." (Courtesy of William Harr.)

The New Galena Inn was rumored to be a "wild place" in the 1920s. Stories about "girls selling their wares" circulated among residents long after the inn burned down while under lease with a motorcycle club in the 1960s. An earthen depression is all that remains today. The sign identifies its location as Levin, the name New Galena held from 1898 until the mid-1920s. (Courtesy of George Pie.)

These two undated views of Piper Tavern, taken approximately 75 years apart, show little change to this famous inn located on Durham Road, Pipersville. Built in 1759, several additions were made between 1784 and 1801 following Col. George Piper's acquisition of the building. Many historical figures such as Benjamin Franklin stopped here while journeying through the colonies. Two centuries later, in the 1940s–1950s, the Piper Tavern attracted so many theater celebrities and distinguished writers that in a *Bucks County Traveler* article, proprietor Bob Brugger worried about the impact these well-known personalities would have on Bucks County's simple country life as a result of their making it "famous." Today this fine-dining establishment still resides in a quiet country setting, just off busy Easton Road (Route 611). (Courtesy of Gregg A. Thomas.)

An interesting historical account exists for the Piper Tavern involving Eva Lear Piper, Colonel Piper's wife, who fearlessly chased off two troublesome Doan Gang compatriots with a sword and flat-iron. Guests included Declaration of Independence signers Benjamin Franklin, Robert Morris, and George Taylor; Marquis de Lafayette; Gen. Thomas Mifflin; Gen. Anthony Wayne; the former king of Spain, Joseph Bonaparte; Dr. Benjamin Rush; and banker Stephen Girard. The original 18th-century structure was rebuilt in 1884. (Courtesy of Gregg A. Thomas.)

Haycock's early-18th-century Mountain House likely accommodated drovers heading to the Philadelphia market as the nearby White Hall Inn was not established until 1850. John Ruth, a late-19th-century researcher, recalled droves commonly comprised of "1000 head of sheep . . . and 150-200 head of steer" being herded along the larger roads such as Old Bethlehem Pike when he was a boy. The hotel was known as Sorrel Horse and then Arianna Miles in more recent times. (Courtesy of Heather Radick, Haycock Historical Society.)

Emil's, formerly the East Rockhill Central Hotel, built around the 1870s, may be the last place in Bucks County still serving "old fashioned oyster pie." The building's one-story section (below on the left) was once a dance hall featuring a player piano (the gas pumps shown were hand-cranked). During Prohibition, bottles of locally made moonshine were hidden in a ground cellar under the porch and also hung into the well by string. A 1950s wall painting (left) by Chief One Star, a poet and Oklahoma Cherokee who painted murals and performed handiwork around taverns for "beer money," remains near the 1930s bar-turned-luncheon counter. Benjamin Franklin Hendricks, who once hopped trains and supervised WPA projects, owned the hotel with his wife, Mamie, from approximately the late 1920s to the 1940s, followed by Albert and Emily Kaupp. Emil Jacoby began his popular "everything from scratch" restaurant here in 1991. (Courtesy of Emil Jacoby.)

Ten years after Jane Housekeeper sold the Globe Hotel to Joseph Kline for $29,000, Quakertown decked itself out for its 1914 chautauqua festival, and so did the Globe. Erected in 1827, the Globe expanded several times following the arrival of the railroad. Up to 32 trains serviced Quakertown daily during its heyday (1890–1920), and the Globe was one of several hotels within short walking distance to lodge travelers. (Courtesy of Gladys Koder.)

In 1825, Enos Schlichter's license petition, accompanied by $1, noted he "kept tavern for some time past where he now resides at the Sign of the Bull's Head." His 1840 renewal application documented the necessity for "accommodation of the public and entertainment of strangers and travelers" along Ridge Road. The village became Schlichterville; the tavern was later called Almont Hotel. Today Fasageo's, Sellersville, entices patrons with its authentic Italian cuisine and cozy pub atmosphere. (Courtesy of Fasageo's; photograph by Tony Bova.)

Don Morris, Point Pleasant's former postmaster, remembers when the late-18th-century Central Hotel (formerly Sutter's) first became Apple Jack's in 1970 it was "a working-man's bar . . . great in hunting season . . . with big meals and plenty of specials." When named the Black Cat in 1937, several patrons adopted the moniker for their motorcycle club. Today patrons enjoy grilled sandwiches, drinks, and camaraderie in Apple Jack's unusual rustic cellar pub. (Courtesy of Lyle Rickards.)

Historian W. W. H. Davis reported in 1876 that the Eagle Hotel, presently the Trum Tavern, dated back to the mid-18th-century and claimed to be "the patriarch of the village" Trumbauersville (formerly Charlestown). Activities related to the Fries Rebellion took place here. A 1904 *Town and Country* newspaper reported the "Spread Eagle" installed an enlarged "mahogany and quartered oak" bar with two beveled wall mirrors and a "nice tile water trough." (Courtesy of Steve Lewis.)

Verna and Paul Hiestand (pictured above center around 1950), owners of Milford Township's Spinnerstown Hotel, were among the first to install a corner mounted television in their bar. In 1959, John and Kate Jenks purchased the business and are seen below celebrating their new venture. While John worked elsewhere laying pipeline, Kate managed the restaurant and tavern (room rentals were discontinued). Kate, like many women in her position, knew how to handle drunken patrons. Described as "90 pounds soaking wet," she once tossed out an offensive member of a motorcycle gang by yanking him to the door by the hair. Eventually the Jenks transitioned management, then ownership, to their informally adopted son John Dale Sr. and his wife, "Sis." They passed the business on to their son John Jr. in 1987. (Courtesy of Susan and John Dale Jr.)

John Ruth's 1897 memoirs noted that Springtown Inn was "a well regulated hostelry where man and beast found excellent accommodation and the sale of intoxicants was not the all important object." It was well known for livestock sales and sponsored events such as the 1892 Shooting Match for Turkeys. Neighbor Alverta Frey reported that a shooting disturbance occurred in 1931, when gangster-types leaving the inn also left a bullet hole in an upstairs bedroom wall of her family home. (Courtesy of Gladys Koder.)

Boating excursions were among several recreational options at Point Pleasant Inn. Some guests relaxed in rockers, canopied gliders, or Adirondack gazebos, while others, including presidents Grover Cleveland and William McKinley, fished on the Delaware River. The more adventurous took countryside carriage rides or walks through the nearby covered bridge and along the Tohickon creek. Today visitors enjoy the unique shopping experience offered by F. P. Kolbe's, a fascinating multiroomed home goods shop in the old hotel. (Courtesy of Rebecca and Richard Kolbe.)

Roads from Easton and Dyers Mill were extended south and north, respectively, to Point Pleasant in 1738. On this road (Ferry Road), Michael Weisel erected the two-story building that became a licensed tavern in 1792. The future Point Pleasant Inn above was reconstructed with a third-story addition in 1812 after a fire. The proprietor Mr. Thompson and his family resided on this level in 1924. The second floor housed guest rooms. C. C. Housem, proprietor of the hotel in the early 20th century, is likely the gentleman at right calling scattered guests with his clanging dinner bell. Being located near seven shad fisheries on the Delaware, not surprisingly, planked shad was a specialty dish here. Historian Willis Rivinus noted that years after closing, "forty well-seasoned oak boards with metal grills" were found in the basement of the present-day F. P. Kolbe's store. (Courtesy of Rebecca and Richard Kolbe.)

Milford Township's Finland Inn (formerly Half-Moon Hotel) served a bustling village that included summer cottages, a sawmill, a gristmill, and a cigar factory in the early 20th century. Although the closest house dates from 1707, little is known about the inn's building other than an addition was made in 1866. Augustus Schuler, proprietor from 1896 to 1906, sponsored a community baseball team and female-led cornet band and was reported to have "started work at his new barroom" in 1903 by *Town and Country* newspaper. Current proprietor Rosanna Kern had decorated this cozy dining establishment with inspired nostalgic touches and was honored in a 1986 flag-raising ceremony by the American Finnish Society for preserving Finland's historic identity (Finland is America's sole community with that name). Kern's family has owned and operated the inn since 1962. Note the gaslight and covered bridge in the above photograph. (Courtesy of Rosanna Hein Kern.)

Originally home to Springfield Township's first miller, Stephen Twining, this beautiful pre-Revolutionary Colonial later housed a tavern purported to be a stopping place for George Washington's soldiers. Sword- and musket-scarred woodwork, a fatal fight between drunken soldiers, and skeletal remains discovered in a walled chimney flue upstairs contribute to the reputation that 18th-century Kuckert's (or Kockert's) Tavern was a raucous hostelry with an intriguing history.

Don Trainer, owner of Quakertown's famous Trainer's Seafood Restaurant, named his Dondormar cocktail lounge and dining room after himself; his wife, Doris; and his mother, Margaret. In 1957, advertisements boasted, "Dining rooms to suit every taste, from formal with organ music and bar, to the old original counter for breakfast and snacks." Multiple rooflines from several expansions hindered firefighters on July 4, 1975, when the building was ravaged and ruined by fire during renovations. (Courtesy of the Quakertown Historical Society.)

The gradual adoption of casual summer apparel in women's fashions is demonstrated in these *c.* 1912 photographs taken at the Point Pleasant Inn, a riverside resort on the Delaware. While the lady above, center, appears painfully uncomfortable in her corset and long-sleeved outfit, the younger women in the photograph below evince future trends. Relaxed hairstyles, shorter sleeves, and sporty sailor garb suggest impending changes in women's fashion. Young ladies would soon dispense with corsets, long hair, and weighty layers of clothing in time for the Roaring Twenties, and their mothers and grandmothers would follow suit. The men pictured, adorned with stiff Arrow collars (available in 400 styles), would eliminate their own restrictive fashion styles in due time. (Courtesy of Rebecca and Richard Kolbe.)

Haycock Township's Strawntown Inn derived its moniker from the village named in honor of the Strawn family. The central section was built for their home in 1710. A descendant converted the building into a tavern around 1750, and subsequent names included Block's Tavern, Long House Tavern, and the Stage Coach Inn. Several additions and more than 250 years after it was first licensed, this former hotel, stage stop, and mail drop still serves the community. Advertised in the 1950s as the place "where celebrities meet," today the Raven's Nest, a local pub and musical venue, holds an annual BluesFest and sponsors dart competitions. It still provides customers, some of whom have been patrons for over 50 years, with a cigarette machine (left), a fast-disappearing relic of the 20th century. (Author's collection.)

Three large murals depicting fox hunts once graced Milford Township's Brick Tavern Inn. Opened as the Spread Eagle in 1818, this hostelry offered "suitable stabling and sheds" at its "large and convenient house" on Old Bethlehem Pike. A general store, post office, and stage stop once existed here, and its large holding pen and weighing scale made it a well-known site for cattle auctions. Steamed clams, "4 doz., $1.00," were a special in 1951. (Courtesy of Barry Riegel.)

Although the owner's earliest handwritten deed for Upper Black Eddys' Indian Rock Inn is dated 1812, the establishment is believed to be older. Situated below the impressive Nockamixon Cliffs along the Delaware canal and river, the former Narrowsville Hotel was a favorite vacation spot for Pres. Grover Cleveland. Once a welcome respite for canal men and stage travelers, this restaurant, bed-and-breakfast, banquet facility, and lively saloon continues to retain its appeal. (Courtesy of the Historic Langhorne Association, Ed Vogenberger Collection.)

Joe Butera, a musician since age 16, started his career as a plastics engineer but found a way to follow his lifelong passion for music by acquiring Gobblers Night Club in Point Pleasant in 1950. This lively oasis in riverside country thrived under Butera's management for over five decades. Here, Butera (on bass) jams with Jack Karpel (piano) and Dick Housel (clarinet) in 1951. (Courtesy of Michael Butera.)

Gobblers frequently featured jazz musicians from New York, such as the Stan Kenton band. Club owner Joe Butera performed on bass every Friday and Saturday night with his own group, the Gobbler's All-Stars. The group performed weekends for patrons from as far away as New York. Gobblers was a popular venue for professional jazz musicians and a favorite local haunt until it was sold in 2004. (Courtesy of Michael Butera.)

Although the Rocket Roller Skating Rink was converted in the early 1930s into an open-air dance pavilion, the Dansant, locals today more fondly recall this building as Gobblers, the restaurant and nightclub operated by Joe Butera for over a half century. Butera's famous "Jazz in Bucks County" Monday night series helped garner a 1976 American Society of Composers, Authors and Publishers (ASCAP) award for featuring 25 continuous years of live music. (Courtesy of Michael Butera.)

In 1950, Joe Butera (behind bar) moved his family from the Chambersburg section of Trenton, New Jersey, to Point Pleasant to operate Gobblers restaurant and nightclub. Butera purchased the business site unseen and turned it into a popular nightspot featuring live jazz, Dixieland music, and Italian cuisine. Local customer Bob McKee is seated at left. (Courtesy of Michael Butera.)

The historically significant Red Lion Hotel, Quakertown's first tavern, began as McCoole's in the mid-18th century and played a part in the Fries Rebellion. A 1950 *Traveler* magazine reported the forerunner of birch beer was a "famous colonial drink" here, its secret formula closely guarded until obtained by a soft drink bottler. Today McCoole's continues to draw customers with "Fine Food & Drink," a warm atmosphere, and weekend entertainment. Although traffic had not changed much from the early to mid-20th century, other things did. When the above trolley was photographed around 1914, the Liberty Bell line was upgrading its standard cars to include "smokers, porters, and carpeted floors," and those newly installed cement sidewalks were surely welcomed after complaints in the late 1890s about the towns' dangerous "plank walks." Note, however, the imprisoned young trees—obviously more innovations were still to come. (Above, courtesy of Gladys Koder; below, courtesy of the Historic Langhorne Association, Ed Vogenberger Collection.)

A gong, whistle, and homemade drum accompanied flag-waving guests who celebrated the Fourth of July, 1912, by forming their own parade while vacationing at the popular Point Pleasant Inn, Tinicum Township. In the 1950s, Frank Kolbe moved his antique store from across the road into the old hotel, attracting pleasure-seeking antique hunters. Today Kolbe's grandson Rich and his wife, Rebecca, operate the eclectic and fun-to-shop F. P. Kolbe's from this once stately edifice. (Courtesy of Rebecca and Richard Kolbe.)

The tavern at Geryville began legally serving spirits in 1745 and was later known as "a resort of the insurgents" during the infamous Fries Rebellion of 1799. It was Conrad Marks's tavern where the "liberators" gathered to march on Bethlehem and free their tax-dissenting compatriots at the Sun Inn. Marks, the tavern's second proprietor, was subsequently called "an atrocious offender" by the judge for his part in the tax revolt and daring raid. The tavern operated under the Sign of the Black Horse for most of the 19th century. The Geryville Hotel sign above is from 1908, while the advertisement below was produced around 1910–1915 before the business closed due to Prohibition. Today a rejuvenated Geryville Publick House is a lively gathering spot, restaurant, and musical venue. (Courtesy of Greg Lepore, photographs by the author.)

The fellows in the above late-19th-to-early-20th-century photograph enjoy their lager in the saloon of L. E. Crouthamel's *c.* 1757 White Horse Hotel on Old Bethlehem Pike, the stage route between Philadelphia and Bethlehem. The pike, formerly the Minsi Trail, is believed to be the oldest road in the United States, having been used by Native Americans before William Penn's time. Today the Horse Tavern and Grill, while only minutes from a busy highway and the Grand View Hospital, maintains its country flavor and its tradition to keep "the lights on, the food good, and the beer cold." (Courtesy of Dave Adelsberger.)

According to local lore, worshippers heading to Schuckenhausen Church in the 1760s would stop at the Pleasant Valley Inn for schnapps passed to them "through the wicket of the quaintly-fashioned bar in generous wide-brimmed seider-al glasses." Seider-al was homemade apple whiskey. In 1790, when temperance supporter Henry Eckel bought the tavern, he had all the spirits dumped into the gutter and turned to making saddlery and harnesses for the army. (Author's collection.)

During a mid-19th-century temperance movement, many of Bucks County's 130 licensed tavern keepers stopped selling spirits under pressure from their communities. Like so many of the others, Henry Beidler, proprietor of the Bulls Head tavern, Springfield Township, stopped serving alcohol on October 1, 1855, following a legislative act controlling intoxicating liquors. The hostelry evolved into the Fairmount Hotel and was later renamed Passer Hotel. It is a private residence today. (Courtesy of Gladys Koder.)

Five years after World War II ended, young and old alike were still whooping it up on New Year's Eve. Party hats, noisemakers, balloons, and confetti were standard accessories, along with fancy drinks and the midnight toast or kiss. Here revelers at the Spinnerstown Hotel celebrate the arrival of the New Year, January 1, 1950. People have been congregating here to conduct business, celebrate, and imbibe at the Spinnerstown tavern for almost two centuries. The property was known for its mid-18th-century distillery that perhaps made mum, a sweet malt liquor then popular with the Germans and sold at Bethlehem. Today Spinnerstown's tastefully decorated restaurant and bar offers over 250 types of ale and lager, 13 beers on tap, and monthly beer tasting nights at Meet the Brewer events. Little wonder customers include those who have been returning for 40–50 years. (Courtesy of Susan and John Dale Jr.)

In 1811, David D. Spinner, son of respected Colonial potter David Spinner whose works reside in several world-famous museums, became the first tavern keeper at Spinnerstown. He lost his tavern license when appointed justice of the peace in 1819. Almost 120 frustrated residents petitioned for "a public house or house of entertainment" under Spinner's tenant John Klein, noting there was no tavern from "Charlestown [Trumbauersville] to Stahler's Tavern," eight to nine miles away. The license was granted in 1822, and today, after almost two centuries of serving the public, the Spinnerstown Hotel has become a destination restaurant and bar under the capable management of third-generation owner John Dale Jr. and his wife, Susan. Although the building now has an enclosed front porch, these photographs show few changes to the front between the early 1900s (above) and 1938 (below). (Courtesy of Susan and John Dale Jr.)

Four

MISCELLANY

Accompanying an early wine glass and champagne bottle are *c.* 1730–1780 reusable black glass spirit bottles. From left to right are a classic English pint beer bottle, an English onion bottle, a *c.* 1760 English case bottle for transporting liquor to taverns, an all-purpose Dutch mallet bottle, the champagne bottle with a manufacturer or family identification seal, another onion bottle, and finally an early Dutch wine bottle. All are from the collection of Iain Haight-Ashton. (Courtesy of Iain Haight-Ashton.)

Although Milford's Finland Inn (above) and Yardley's Continental Hotel (below) retained their 19th-century wood- and coal-fueled cast-iron stoves for cooking, baking, and probably heating, "modern" gas ranges had arrived by the 1920s. Just as cooks once transitioned from open-hearth cooking and beehive oven baking, practice on these new appliances was necessary to become proficient at turning out a good meal. The electric lights were probably an early-20th-century addition, although covered overhead fixtures had not yet been adopted. The Finland Inn and the Continental Tavern each have a welcoming restaurant and tavern serving the public today. (Above, courtesy of Rosanna Kern; below, courtesy of Frank Lyons.)

As the local tavern was once the only public edifice other than a house of worship that accommodated large gatherings, they were frequently used for community events and entertainment. Today sports teams, business associations, fraternal groups, and other large organizations meet regularly in such environs. These unidentified Girl Scouts and their troop leaders in the 1940s are attending an event at Flannery's, Penndel. (Courtesy of the Historic Langhorne Association.)

In the days before air-conditioning, the Langhorne Hotel promoted itself to patrons by presenting this colorful cardboard fan with a quixotic Native American image. Embossed matchbooks, ashtrays, glasses, lighters, bottle openers, thermometers, and even switchblades and night lights were among advertising items distributed in 20th-century taverns and hotels. Such pieces have become collectors' items. (Courtesy of the Historic Langhorne Association.)

This Brick Tavern "monument" is what remains of an actual turnpike. After toll collections were discontinued in Milford Township on Old Bethlehem Pike, the pike was removed and the relic became a trolley stop marker. The Barley Sheaf, as the tavern was known through most of the 19th century, had also been an Underground Railroad stop. Barry Riegel, proprietor from 1982 to 2005, remembered a tunnel (which hid illegal liquor during Prohibition) collapsing during road construction. (Author's collection.)

In 1935, shortly after Prohibition ended, the Old Mr. Boston "official bartender's guide" was circulated to promote its brand of alcohol. Hundreds of concoctions for Old Mr. Boston whiskey, gin, rum, brandy, bourbon, and cordials were included. Recipes to make old-fashioned flips, toddies, and punches could be found alongside those for highballs, swizzles, fizzes, and slings. Americans could now, finally, treat themselves to a Tailspin Cocktail or a Brandy Smash legally. (Courtesy of the Historic Langhorne Association.)

The Wilson Distillery Company, a whiskey supplier, purchased Bristol's vacant patent leather company building in April 1937. Wilson's was established in 1823 in New York and originally known as Brown Vitner's. Upon relocation to Bristol, the company projected it would employ 275 people—three-quarters female. Ninety-two-year-old resident Joe Cuttone recalls the company closing following World War II after struggling with persistent product theft. The building was demolished around 2007. (Courtesy of Joseph Cuttone.)

During the late 19th century, gentlemen were expected to be above spitting on the floor, and so spittoons became common at taverns and other male gathering places. Some public houses added a spit trough at the base of the bar with a drain and spigot to wash away the discarded chew tobacco and expectorate. During Spinnerstown Hotel renovations, this decoratively tiled trough was enclosed, a remnant of the days before public health regulations. (Courtesy of Susan and John Dale Jr.)

Monastic hostels serving pilgrims in 14th-century England often adapted names alluding to religious references, such as Cross Keys, for St. Peters emblem. The Cross Keys name was used in the 1758 license application for the Cross Keys Tavern located in Plumstead near the Doylestown boundary line. Frank and Emily Conti purchased the place around 1943–1944, launching the successful Conti Inn (cocktail napkin shown). The Cross Keys building has sat vacant since Conti's closed in 1995. (Courtesy of Walter Conti.)

This timeworn Colonial coaching horn, used to announce the approach of the stagecoach, generated great activity among those who could hear its blast. Tavern keepers and the help scurried to prepare for weary travelers, while locals anticipated the arrival of guests, delivery packets, mail, and news from afar. Dogs barked, and children eagerly ran to observe all the excitement. When the stage arrived, the day came alive.

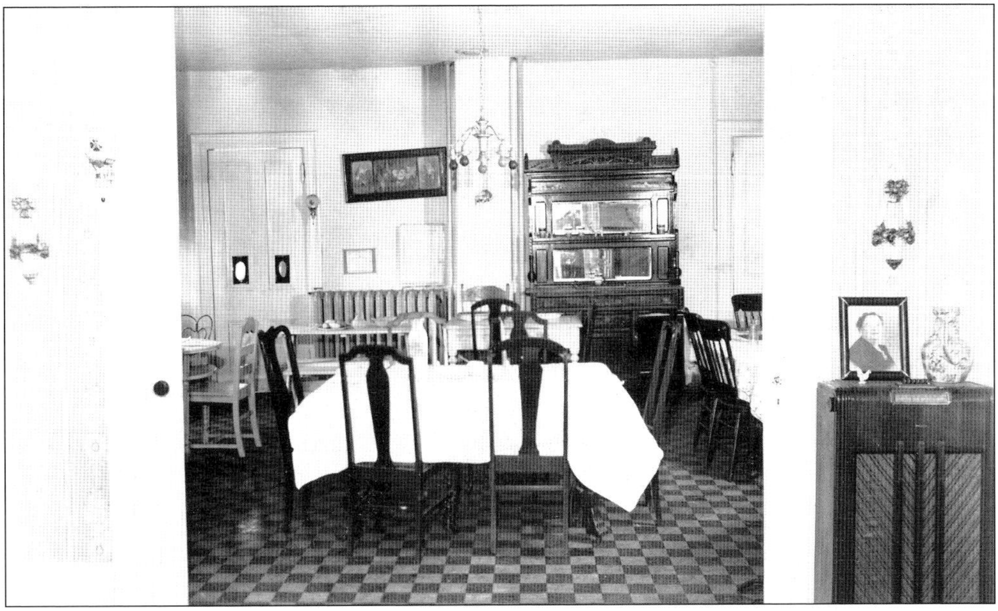

These views of two different Bucks County establishments demonstrate the type of change undergone by many places in the mid-20th century. The 1940s dining room of Yardley's Continental Tavern, above, still sports furniture from the early 1900s, a linoleum floor, and cast-iron radiators, all of which were still common when this photograph was taken. Post–World War II prosperity fostered modernization, and by the 1960s the swirled carpet, knotty pine paneling, and blond furniture seen in the air-conditioned dining room of Conti Inn, below, were the epitome of stylish decor. Conti's has since been replaced by a gas station and convenience store, while the Continental Tavern has undergone stylish renovation and renewal under new ownership. (Above, courtesy of Frank Lyons; below, courtesy of Walter Conti.)

This assortment of 1680–1780 Dutch and early-American brass candlesticks are typical of those that sat on tables in finer Colonial Bucks County taverns. The chamber stick, front left, would have hung by the fireplace before being lighted and used to guide guests up dark stairs to their rooms. The center *c.* 1750 English wick trimmer is bounded by two late-17th-century English wick trimmers. All are from the collection of Iain Haight-Ashton. (Courtesy of Iain Haight-Ashton.)

This long-handled, perforated tin candle cover was used in a regional tavern. Both decorative and functional, its design emitted light while protecting the flame from common drafts and contact with people and flammable objects.

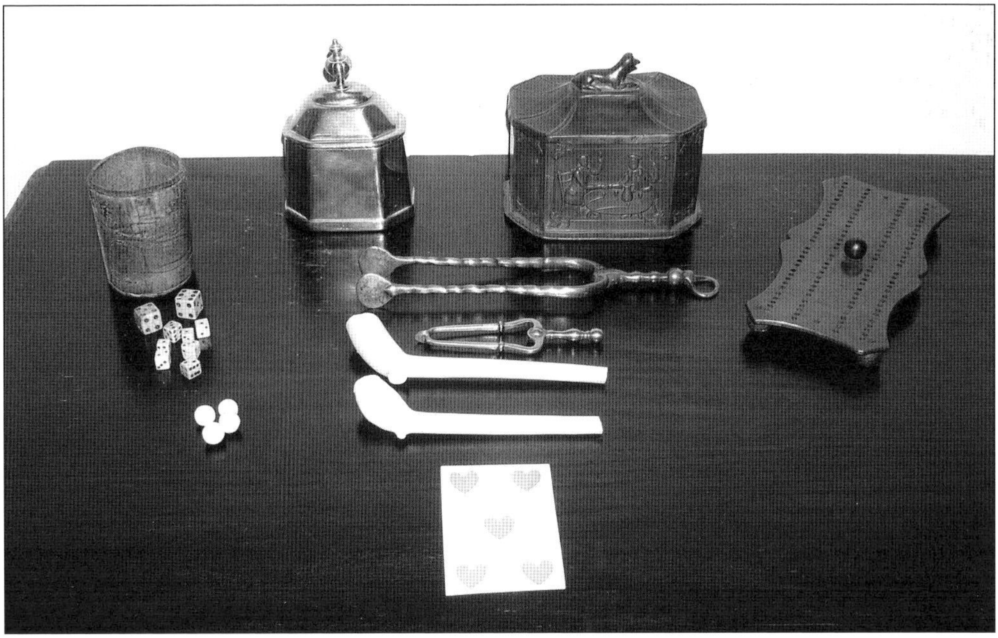

Above are various items from different classes of Colonial taverns. In the rear are a c. 1750 brass tobacco box and rare c. 1770 pewter tobacco box. Below them are "amber tongs," the larger for transporting coals to a plate warmer and the smaller for lighting clay pipes such as the two beneath. The leather shaker, dice, and playing card would likely have been used for betting in the back room of a tavern. At the far right is a cribbage board. This tobacco box from Iain Haight-Ashton's collection retains its original damper, a flat piece of lead used as a press to keep the tobacco moist. An animal figure used as a lid knob was a common tobacco box feature. (Courtesy of Iain Haight-Ashton.)

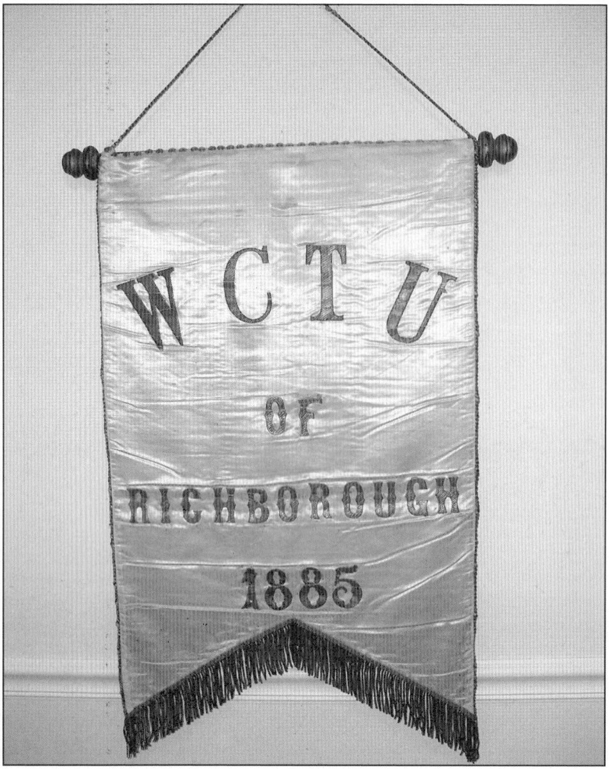

The Women's Christian Temperance Union, established in 1874, is self-described as "the oldest continuing non-sectarian woman's organization in the world." Early temperance advocates marched on saloons to stop alcohol sales and abuse. Since no legal protections existed, abstinence was demanded to provide increased security to women and children, the frequent victims of alcohol misuse by others. The Women's Christian Temperance Union has since helped establish many rights for women. This banner belonged to Northampton's Elcie Bennett Cornell. (Courtesy of Betty Luff.)

This 1772 bronze tavern pint measure was typical of those required to be kept in plain view by law. Periodically the crown official responsible for weights and measure would visit a tavern and order a beer without identifying himself. He then poured the beer from his mug into this measure to ensure it met standards requirements. If not, the tavern was fined for violation. This measure is in the collection of Iain Haight-Ashton. (Courtesy of Iain Haight-Ashton.)

These Colonial-era tavern mugs from the collection of Iain Haight-Ashton include two German Westerwald jugs made for the English market. The initials on the *c.* 1710 jug, far left, stand for Queen Anne; the other, far right, around 1750, for King George II—both signify loyalty toward the crown. The *c.* 1760 Japanese Amari porcelain tankard, second from left, stands next to a late-18th-to-early-19th-century pewter mug. The 1760–1770 "Ale" mug is English creamware. (Courtesy of Iain Haight-Ashton.)

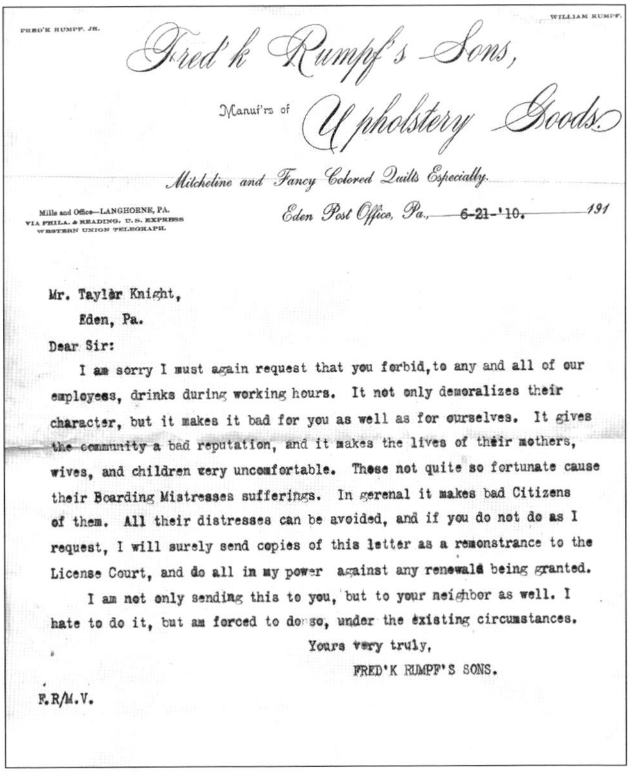

FRED'K RUMPF, JR. WILLIAM RUMPF.

Fred'k Rumpf's Sons,

Manuf'rs of *Upholstery Goods.*

Mitcheline and Fancy Colored Quilts Especially.

Mills and Office—LANGHORNE, PA.
VIA PHILA. & READING. U. S. EXPRESS
WESTERN UNION TELEGRAPH.

Eden Post Office, Pa., 6-21-'10. *191*

Mr. Taylòr Knight,
Eden, Pa.

Dear Sir:

I am sorry I must again request that you forbid, to any and all of our employees, drinks during working hours. It not only demoralizes their character, but it makes it bad for you as well as for ourselves. It gives the community a bad reputation, and it makes the lives of their mothers, wives, and children very uncomfortable. These not quite so fortunate cause their Boarding Mistresses sufferings. In gerenal it makes bad Citizens of them. All their distresses can be avoided, and if you do not do as I request, I will surely send copies of this letter as a remonstrance to the License Court, and do all in my power against any renewals being granted.

I am not only sending this to you, but to your neighbor as well. I hate to do it, but am forced to do so, under the existing circumstances.

Yours very truly,
FRED'K RUMPF'S SONS.

F.R/M.V.

Tavern owners received pleading letters from wives, daughters, sisters, and even employers asking them to stop serving "strong drink" to particular tippling customers. Some threatened prosecution "according to the law," hoping the power of the license court would gain cooperation. This letter writer cited harm done to wives, children, and "boarding mistresses" as a result of too much imbibing and requested the Langhorne House not serve alcohol to his employees. (Courtesy of the Historic Langhorne Association.)

Stage travelers determined distance between stops by mileposts. Rudolf P. Hommel, a Pleasant Valley resident in the 1930s and 1940s, saved many of these relics while tracing the original artery from Philadelphia to Bethlehem. After restoring the markers, including this one in Upper Bucks County, Hommel had them reset by the state. In the 1920s, Hommel collected items in China for his esteemed friend, Dr. Henry Mercer, Bucks County Historical Society. (Author's collection.)

Prior to the automobile, a livery stable adjacent to a hotel was as necessary to a traveler with a horse as a parking garage is today. A blacksmith, the mechanic of his day, was often located nearby. Not surprisingly, this livery shed behind the Spinnerstown Hotel expanded to become a service garage once automobiles came to rule the day. The second floor was used for dances and other community events. (Courtesy of Susan and John Dale Jr.)

Women's groups such as the Bucks Country Federation of Women's Clubs supported communities throughout Bucks and helped save many historical buildings. This ladies' club raised funds to restore and purchase period furnishings for Taylorsville's Old Ferry Inn (also known as McKonkey's) and was being honored by the state for its work when this photograph was taken in April 1966. George Washington dined at this inn before embarking on the Battle of Trenton with his troops on Christmas 1776. (Courtesy of Washington Crossing Historic Park, Pennsylvania Historical and Museum Commission.)

Consistent with our mission to preserve history on a local level, this book was printed in South Carolina on American-made paper and manufactured entirely in the United States. Products carrying the accredited Forest Stewardship Council (FSC) label are printed on 100 percent FSC-certified paper.

MADE IN THE USA